BRONTË IN LOVE

SARAH FREEMAN

GREAT NORTHERN

Great Northern Books
PO Box 213, Ilkley, LS29 9WS
www.greatnorthernbooks.co.uk

© Sarah Freeman, 2010.

Except where otherwise credited, all illustrations are from Yorkshire Post Newspapers. Those on pages 17 (top), 50, 74, 100, 106, 127, 151, 154, 159 and 182 are of exhibits at the Brontë Parsonage Museum.

ISBN: 978 1 905080 70 0

Design and layout: David Burrill

CIP Data
A catalogue for this book is available from the British Library

BRONTË IN LOVE

SARAH FREEMAN

GREAT NORTHERN

Contents

*Charlotte Brontë brought to life by JH Thompson whose painting
was based on George Richmond's original portrait of the author.
(© The Brontë Society)*

FOREWORD

by Kay Mellor OBE

Brontë in Love looks at the life of one of English Literature's greatest female novelists. When Charlotte Brontë was born on April 21, 1816, there was no great fanfare. Moving to the parsonage at Haworth when she was just three-years-old, her childhood appeared no different from that of countless other girls growing up in the Church in 19th century England.

While an avid reader and undeniably bright, ambition was a luxury reserved only for those with money and connections. The Brontë family had neither, yet out of these ordinary origins an extraordinary talent did finally emerge.

Much has been written about the Brontë sisters, but Charlotte is still too often cast as the hopeless romantic who spent her life quietly wandering the Yorkshire moors never troubling anyone and who only expressed her passion and fiery emotions about heartbreak and madness through her writing. When you read Brontë in Love you realise this is an absolute myth and the greatest love story Charlotte never told was her own. Sarah Freeman tells that story. She uncovers the truth about Charlotte's life — she excavates the force that compelled Charlotte to write; the great loves in her life, her vulnerability, her courage and her tragic sufferings. We are left in no doubt that Charlotte Brontë was a complicated, intelligent woman who had the highest of standards. She was a woman who dared to stand out in an era where conformity was king.

By the time of her death, Charlotte's love life rivalled that of any of her heroines. She knew what it meant to be the victim of unrequited love, she had flirted with romance and she had twice nursed the pain of a broken heart.

The book is an absolute page-turner. I defy anyone to put it down. Not only will you enjoy Brontë in Love, but having read it, you will want to revisit Jane Eyre, Shirley and Villette. It will add a greater depth and make the stories all the more fascinating and poignant. Sarah Freeman knows how to tell a story just as compelling as Charlotte told hers. And so 'Reader'....enjoy.

1. Passion Ignited

"To fear love is to fear life, and those who fear life are already three parts dead."
(Bertrand Russell)

Charlotte Brontë desperately wanted to believe that brains were more important than beauty. Yet whenever she looked in the mirror or caught a glimpse of herself in one of the windows of her home in Haworth parsonage, she couldn't help but feel disappointed.

She was short. Her lips were too small. Her head was far too big for her thin body. As for her hair, when curled it looked dry and frizzy; when left to its own devices it sat limply round her bony shoulders.

Charlotte was her own harshest critic. Her heart beat more passionately than anyone she had ever known, but she felt trapped within the plainest of exteriors. Blind to her simple, understated beauty, she spent much of her life wishing to be different. She wanted to be taller, prettier and more elegant. Charlotte blamed her tiny frame and physical frailness on the time she had spent at the Clergy Daughters' School in Cowan Bridge. She had been sent there by her father with the very best intentions when she was just eight-years-old, but it proved one of the unhappiest times of her life. The children were seen by many of the teaching staff as little more than a necessary evil, the food was often inedible and the unsanitary conditions were a breeding ground for disease. It was there Charlotte's two elder sisters, Maria and Elizabeth, caught a fatal case of tuberculosis and while she returned home after ten months, she believed the damage had already been done.

As she grew older she found much else to complain about in her appearance. The glasses she needed to correct her poor eyesight made her look prematurely old and as her friend Mary Taylor once remarked, her short-sightedness meant she "always seemed to be seeking something."

For Charlotte, her appearance was a constant reminder of the unfairness of real life and from the earliest age it forced a retreat into imaginary worlds where the heart always ruled the head and where those who loved passionately almost always triumphed. These were worlds unpolluted by industrial chimneys which belched out smoke and noxious gases; worlds where beauty wasn't a prerequisite to success and where love conquered all.

Most of those who found themselves invited into the Haworth parsonage with its bare sandstone floors and grey painted walls would have found little to hold their interest for very long. It was to all but the most careful observer the kind of existence where each day was the same as the next and where life brought few surprises. Visitors may have caught a glimpse of the local art tutor hired to instruct the Brontë children in painting and drawing. They may have heard musical scales being practised on the small piano or seen Patrick Brontë, a man whose own humble beginnings had shown him the value of education, teaching his children the basics of maths

As a child, Charlotte was a prolific writer and a talented artist. Her tiny books were populated by strong men and glamorous women, including the Zenobia Marchioness Ellrington who she drew here. (courtesy of the Brontë Society)

and geography. Born to a hard-working Irish farming family, Patrick had seen his own parents struggle and had grown determined not to follow in their footsteps. By the time he was sixteen-years-old he had opened his own school and having decided to enter the Church seven years later, he won a place at Cambridge University. It was an achievement which spoke volumes about his ambition.

Learning to Patrick was everything and his children inherited his voracious appetite for knowledge. When formal lessons were over, Charlotte, her two younger sisters Emily and Anne and brother Branwell reached for one of the many books which lined the shelves on either side of the dining room fireplace. Almost immediately their otherwise grey world was transformed. Turning the pages of *Paradise Lost* and *The Pilgrim's Progress*, the four surviving Brontë children discovered lands much brighter and more optimistic than the one which lay outside their own front door. With Patrick of the firm belief that curtains were an unnecessary fire risk, it was impossible to shut out the days when dark rain clouds hung heavy on the moors or when the sun tried to scorch its own impression on the bricks and mortar, but through books Charlotte found an escape. She may have never gone much beyond the edge of the moors above Haworth, but as she read of adventures in foreign lands she was taken on much greater flights of fancy.

It was little wonder Charlotte craved a world of exciting possibilities, where happy endings could be delivered at a stroke of a pen and where old enemies could be dispatched with similar efficiency. Aside from her own feelings of physical inferiority, which often crippled her in the company of others, by the time she had celebrated her ninth birthday, she had lost not only her elder sisters but also her mother.

For those growing up in the heart of the industrial north, sickness and disease were never far away. In Haworth, where the average life expectancy was twenty-five, measles, whooping cough and tuberculosis were rife. With the town devoid of an efficient sewerage system, pools of stagnant water were a familiar sight on the streets and a putrid river of waste from the local slaughterhouse washed over the cobbles. Outside the parsonage the grim reality of life in a textile town may have been all too evident, but inside the collective daydreams of the Brontë family took them to lands where no-one needed to scratch a living combing wool and where mortality statistics were unimportant.

As dusk turned to night, the children would often listen wide-eyed to their servant Tabitha Aykroyd, known affectionately as Tabby, as she regaled them with tales of a time before the mills and factories had arrived. It was a time, she told them, when fairies inhabited the same moors where they now spent many happy hours playing. Occasionally, their father would emerge from his study and tell them stories of strange people in strange lands, which his parishioners had sworn were true. Charlotte's imagination was awakened and when her father presented Branwell with a box of toy soldiers it inspired a passion for storytelling and romance which would become all-consuming. Having each chosen one of the models as leader, the four children created their own islands. Each had its own rules and regulations and its own heroes and villains. It was what Charlotte would come to call their "world below". It was where she would retreat whenever she felt lost and lonely and it was where she would later turn when the men she gave her heart refused to repay in kind.

Whenever the door was closed to both the elements and the steady stream of visiting clergymen and parishioners, and when the

Today the cobbles of Haworth are a quaint reminder of a time long gone, but when Charlotte was growing up the town's streets were often covered by an unpleasant mix of water and sewage.

daily chores were done, the rooms of Haworth parsonage became populated by heroes who always got their way and heroines who more often than not were happy to comply. While their father was occupied in his study, the only sign of his presence the smell of tobacco smoke as it wafted across the hallway, Charlotte, Emily, Branwell and Anne found an outlet for their smouldering imaginations.

As the months passed, the children split off into pairs. Anne and Elizabeth formed their own fictional world of Gondal and it was in Glass Town and later in the exotic land they called Angria that Charlotte and Branwell let their own imaginations run riot.

Away from the prying eyes of the practical and the pragmatic, they wrote countless adventures about the exploits of great soldiers and their vicious enemies. They plotted battles, dished out cruel revenge and Charlotte sketched out the rules of romance which would govern much of the rest of her life. Writing in the tiniest of handwriting and read by no-one else but her three siblings, she found a freedom which real life was unlikely ever to offer a 4ft 9ins, short-sighted daughter of a humble cleric. In Angria anything was possible.

Inspired by the likes of the irrepressible Lord Byron, the romanticism of William Wordsworth and the stories she had read about the Duke of Wellington, the military statesman who had defeated Napoleon in the Battle of Waterloo, her early fairytales soon turned into torrid romances. Behind her plain clothes the teenage Charlotte was just waking up and her hopes and dreams became embodied in the swashbuckling rogues and temptresses of Angria. Of all the characters Charlotte brought to life, the Duke of Zamorna, the ultimate embodiment of raw machismo, revealed the most about her burning passion. "There he stood with the red firelight flashing over him," she wrote in one of the many instalments infused by the sound of her fast beating heart. "One foot advanced, his head proudly raised, his kindled eyes fixed on the opposite wall and filled with the most inspired glory."

Zamorna was cruel. He was masterful. He was domineering. He also had two wives, an illegitimate child, numerous mistresses and lived a life full of political intrigue and bloody feuds. Few would have suspected the girl who every night dutifully knelt down to say her prayers and who spent Sunday mornings, head bowed, in the pews of Haworth church, listening to her father preach about moral goodness, could have been capable of such graphic portrayals.

This erotic and passionate world was as real to Charlotte as the stone walls of the parsonage, and it was one over which she crucially had complete control. Angria and the relationships Charlotte made and broke there became an obsession. By the time she turned seventeen, she had written more words than she would during the whole of the rest of her life. To her father, the hours Charlotte spent crouched over her journals were nothing more than a sign of a creative mind occupying itself. Had he ever bothered to decipher the miniature script, he would have discovered a girl whose heart was already on fire; a hopeless romantic who refused to let reality temper her idealism. While Charlotte was aware of the long hours and poor working conditions experienced by many of those who lived just a few hundred yards away, in Angria she was more than happy to shut her eyes to such harsh existence.

When not in the parsonage chatting excitedly with her three siblings about the latest developments in their imaginary worlds, the four could be found walking on the moors behind the house. Navigating their way between the stone quarries, the children rarely saw another soul and with visits to the centre of town both rare and brief, Charlotte's wild train of thought was allowed to run uninterrupted. It was just the way she liked it.

In Angria, she alone determined the course of romance, she gave voice to whatever came into her mind and with no one to tell her she was sinful and wicked she passed off her own stirring passion as belonging to some wanton fictional character.

Unlike Angria, Haworth offered few eligible bachelors. Most had no option but to join the recruits of the hard-working and low paid from an early age and marriage was just another step on an often all too short journey through a life overshadowed by tragedy and heartache. Unlike Charlotte, the wool workers of Haworth had neither the time, the inclination nor the education to immerse themselves in classic literature which fuelled her own desires. For them the pursuit of true love was a luxury none could afford. For the most part Charlotte kept her romantic notions to herself, well aware, perhaps, her fantasies would be dismissed as the silly daydreams of a young girl who knew no better. However, just occasionally she was unable to hold her tongue. When others were often least expecting it, her desire for a destiny other than the one that seemed to have been mapped out for her found a voice.

"I should for once like to feel out and out a schoolgirl; I wish something would happen!" her lifelong friend Ellen Nussey remembered Charlotte saying as they spent their last day together at Roe Head School, where she had been sent by her father to get the rudimentary education which would set her on the path to becoming a governess. "Let us run around the fruit garden; perhaps we shall meet someone or we may have a fine for trespass."

It was an unlikely outburst from a girl who had arrived at the

From the earliest of ages, Charlotte's tiny handwriting filled countless books as she found escape from the realities of life through fiction. (courtesy of the Brontë Society)

school aged just fourteen, but looking to the other pupils like a little old woman and who spent whatever free time she had with her nose pressed up against a book, rarely bothering to raise her head when others asked her to join in some new game.

However, unbeknown to everyone besides her brothers and sisters, Charlotte was already leading a dangerous double life. To those that taught her, she was an able student, often top of the class, but her true brilliance was often hidden by reticence. To the parishioners of Haworth she was a devoted clergyman's daughter, who had learnt the lessons of the Bible well. To many of her fellow students at Roe Head, she was a loner. Serious, hardworking, she lacked any lightness of character to make her easily likeable. However, her shy smile hid a multitude of emotions which the well-bred but poor were not supposed to feel. The gap between her Christian duty and her inner thoughts troubled Charlotte little as a child, but as she grew up the gulf fed a real sense of anxiety. She knew how she was supposed to behave, but she also knew the emotions which bubbled underneath could not be ignored.

"If I could always live with you and daily read the Bible with you," she wrote to Ellen, not long after she had been asked by Margaret Wooler, the headmistress of Roe Head, to return to the school as a teacher. She had just turned nineteen, but she was already well aware her wild imagination jarred with all the lessons she had been taught on how to lead a good Christian life.

"Don't deceive yourself by imagining that I have a bit of real goodness about me. My darling if I were like you I should have my face Zionward through prejudice and error might occasional fling a mist over the glorious vision before me for with all your single-hearted sincerity you have your faults. But I am not like you.

"If you knew my thoughts; the dreams that absorb me; and the fiery imagination that at times eats me up and makes me feel Society as it is, wretchedly insipid, you would pity and I dare say despise me. But Ellen I know the treasures of the Bible, I love and adore them, I can see the Well of Life in all its clearness and brightness, but when I stoop down to drink of the pure waters they fly from my lips as if I were Tantalus. I have written like a fool. Remember me to your Mother and Sister....Come and see me soon; don't think me mad, this is a silly letter."

Ellen, the thirteenth and youngest child of a Yorkshire cloth manufacturer, did her best to set her friend on the path to righteousness, but the advice fell on deaf ears. Charlotte simply couldn't convince herself to accept a life of quiet servitude. She wanted more. Much more.

"If your lips and mine could at the same time, drink the same draught from the same pure fountain of Mercy," she wrote again to Ellen. "I hope, I trust, I might one day become better, far better, than my evil wandering thoughts, my corrupt heart, cold to the spirit and warm to the flesh will now permit me to be. If I could always live with you and daily read the bible with you. If Christian perfection be necessary to Salvation I shall never be saved, my heart is a red hot bed for sinful thoughts and as to practice, when I decide on action I scarcely remember to look to my Redeemer for direction. I know not how to pray, I cannot bind my life to the grand end of doing good. I go on constantly seeking my own pleasure, pursuing the gratification of my own desires, I forget God and will not God forget me?...I adore the purity of the Christian faith, my theory is right, my practice horribly wrong."

As Charlotte passed through her teens and into her twenties, her romantic view of life refused to be confined to the secret pages of her Angria journals. She could keep silent no more.

While other women of her age and class were resigned to bowing to the wishes of fathers, brothers and husbands, Charlotte wanted none of it. She believed her thoughts, her feelings and the poems they had given birth to were equal to that of any man and deserved a public audience. Despite having little life experience, in one of those moments when passion overtook her sense of duty, she set about trying to attract the attention of one of the country's most influential literary figures. Robert Southey was Britain's poet laureate and among the many letters he received from aspiring writers during 1837 was one bearing a Haworth postmark. Enclosing a letter of introduction and a selection of her poems, Charlotte waited eagerly for a reply. When it came, the response was not what she wanted to hear. While Southey, a serious thinker with an appearance to suit, confessed she had talent, he made it clear that any idea she could become a published author was a romantic notion best forgotten. If she didn't lower her expectations and stop striving for the impossible, her life, he said, would be one constant series of disappointments.

"You evidently possess, and in no inconsiderable degree, what Wordsworth calls the 'faculty of verse'…but it is not with a view to distinction that you should cultivate this talent, if you consult your own happiness…The day dreams in which you habitually indulge are likely to induce a distempered state of mind; and, in proportion as all the ordinary uses of the world seem to you flat and unprofitable, you will be unfitted for them without becoming fitted for anything else. Literature cannot be the business of a woman's life and it ought not to be. The more she is engaged in her proper duties, the less leisure she will have for it, even as an accomplishment and a recreation. To those duties you have not yet been called and when you are you will be less eager for celebrity."

He couldn't have been more candid. Charlotte had been told to put aside thoughts of writing critically acclaimed poetry and prose. She had been advised to ignore the foolish ramblings of her heart and instead concentrate on finding a decent, if not necessarily exciting, husband. She should think less about the Duke Zamorna and more about the cooking and the cleaning. Given the courage she had already shown in sending off her work, it was perhaps no surprise that she couldn't resist having the final word. With her tongue firmly in her cheek, she told Southey that having taken on board his warm words of advice, she would in the future try to take much greater delight in sewing and should ambition ever dare to raise its ugly head again, she would read his letter and remind herself of her allotted place in life.

While the poet laureate may have been dismissive, his appraisal was in truth an honest one. Brains were not a valuable currency to a mid 19th century parson's daughter and while Charlotte was not alone in going to sleep dreaming of foreign lands and romantic heroes, most woke up resigned to getting on with the more mundane business of life. Even her father had learnt that particular lesson.

His marriage to Charlotte's mother, Maria Branwell, had by all accounts been a happy one. She had given him six children in seven years and the letters she'd written to him during their courtship brimmed with genuine affection. However, when she died from cancer when Charlotte was just five-years-old, the practical need of finding a carer and housekeeper for his large family saw Patrick

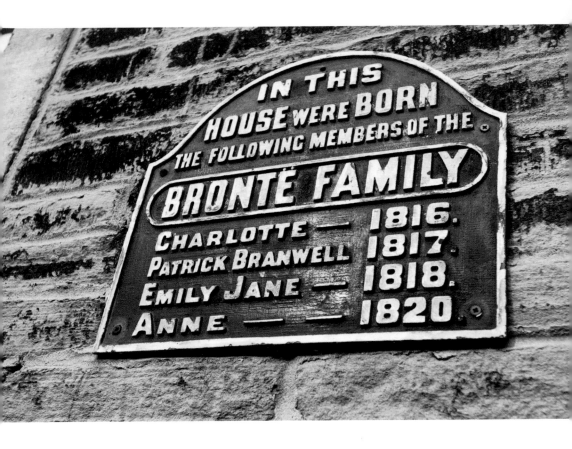

The parsonage was the place Charlotte called home, but she was born a few miles away in Thornton. Today a commemorative plaque marks her birthplace.

quickly return to the marriage market. It was the kind of practical approach, devoid of any emotion other than desperation, that Charlotte herself would never have been able to sanction.

Having mentally scrolled through a list of potential wives, he first wrote to Elizabeth Firth, who had been his neighbour when the Brontë family had lived in nearby Thornton some years earlier. On paper she seemed like an ideal match. Elizabeth was already a family friend so he knew she was of good character and living just a few miles away, if she agreed to become the second Mrs Brontë the cost of transporting whatever worldly goods she had would be minimal. Unfortunately for Charlotte's father, Elizabeth did not share his no-nonsense optimism and politely but firmly turned down the proposal.

Patrick didn't take long to get over the rejection. A few weeks later he had a brainwave, even more staggering in its insensitivity than his offer to Elizabeth Firth. As a young curate in Essex, a few years before he met Maria, Patrick had fallen in love and become engaged to his landlady's niece. Mary Burder was an eligible young woman, but the courtship had ended abruptly. Some said her family disapproved of the relationship. Others thought Patrick had got cold feet and jilted his fiancée. Whatever the truth of the affair, finding himself once again single, he decided to find out whether absence had made Mary's heart grow fonder.

"I experienced a very agreeable sensation in my heart at this moment on reflecting that you are still single, and am so selfish as to wish you to remain so, even if you would never allow me to see you," he wrote in a letter which talked much of emotion, but felt of little.

"You were the first whose hand I solicited, and no doubt I was the first to whom you promised to give that hand…It is now almost fifteen years since I last saw you. This is a long interval of time and may have effected many changes. It has made me look something older. But, I trust I have gained more than I have lost, I hope I may venture to say I am wiser and better…I have a small but sweet little family that often soothe my heart, and afford me pleasure by their endearing little ways, and I have what I consider a competency of the good things in life…I want but one addition to my comforts, and then I think I should wish for no more on this side of eternity. I want to see a dearly Beloved Friend, kind as I once saw her, and as much disposed to promote my happiness…I cannot tell how you may feel on reading this, but I must say my ancient love is rekindled, and I have a longing desire to see you."

Mary was in no mood to be wooed.

"My present condition upon which you are pleased to remark has hitherto been the state of my choice and to me a state of much happiness and comfort," she wrote, the tone as sharp as the pen nib. "I have the kindest and most indulgent parents, sisters and brothers, no domestic cares and anxieties; no husband to control or oppose me…I feel no willingness to risk in a change so many enjoyments in possession…The Lord can supply all your and their need."

Had Charlotte ever been made aware of her father's desperate attempts to secure a wife, she would have quietly applauded Mary's principled stance against a man clearly more interested in finding himself a housemaid and a nanny than a wife. Patrick was not peculiar in his approach to domestic bliss. Marriages of convenience were the norm, but as everyone knew they usually ended in a life of abject inconvenience for either the husband, the wife and usually both. When Patrick's sister-in-law Elizabeth Branwell agreed to move from Cornwall to Yorkshire to look after her nieces and nephew, Patrick breathed a sigh of relief and put aside any further thoughts of marriage. Having taken care of the needs of his children, he was destined to remain single and so it seemed for very different reasons was Charlotte.

While the men of Haworth hadn't exactly fallen at the feet of the parson's daughter, there were offers which others, less resolute in the belief and pursuit of true love, would have happily embraced. Shortly before her twenty-third birthday, Charlotte received her first proposal of marriage. It was a joyless affair, for sadly Henry Nussey wasn't cut from the same romantic cloth as his intended. The brother of Charlotte's friend Ellen, Henry had recently graduated from Cambridge University and had found himself as a curate in Sussex in desperate need of a wife.

The two had met a number of times when Charlotte had visited the Nussey family home. However, his presence had never added to the real joy of seeing Ellen and the little she had gleaned about him through their unmemorable conversations had done nothing to improve her opinion of him.

Henry didn't know an awful lot about Charlotte either, but this wasn't intended to be a lavish proposal or a heart-rending confession of just how much he loved her. No, Henry was a conventional man and he formally set down his intentions in a brief letter.

Knowing Charlotte was unlikely to be inundated with offers, his proposal may have been bland, it may have lacked the customary flattery, but nevertheless it was, he told himself, a good one. Certainly it was a passport to financial security and for the very first time Charlotte, who had talked so long of the necessity of true love and the irrelevance of marriage without it, had to put her romantic principles to the test. They passed easily.

Written in the same tone he might have used to ask a colleague to cover a Sunday service or a parishioner to tidy up the hymn books, Henry's letter didn't trouble Charlotte's heart with even the briefest of flutters. It wasn't a proposal of marriage, it was a business deal from which she was sure she could never profit. Her independence was worth more than a few extra shillings a year and there was no need to wonder whether in time they could make a marriage work. Henry was no husband for Charlotte and she immediately told him so.

"My Dear Sir," she began. "Before answering your letter I might have spent a long time in consideration of its subject; but as from the first moment of its reception and perusal I determined on what course to pursue, it seemed to me that delay was wholly unnecessary." Charlotte was nothing if not blunt. "You are aware that I have many reasons to feel grateful to your family, that I have peculiar reasons for affection towards one at least of your sisters, and also that I highly esteem yourself – do not therefore accuse me of wrong motives when I say that my answer to your proposal must be a decided negative. In forming this decision, I trust I have listened to the dictates of conscience more than to those of inclination. I have no personal repugnance to the idea of a union with you, but I feel convinced that mine is not the sort of disposition calculated to form the happiness of a man like you. It has always been my habit to study the characters of those amongst whom I chance to be thrown and I think I know yours and can imagine what description of woman would suit you for a wife. The character should not be too marked, ardent and original, her temper should be mild, her piety undoubted, her spirits even and cheerful, and her personal suppressing my rage at the idleness, the apathy and the hyperbolical and most asinine stupidity of these fat headed oafs, and of compulsion assuming an air of kindness, patience and assiduity? Must I from day to day sit chained to this chair, prisoned within these four bare walls, while these glorious summer suns are burning in heaven and the year is revolving in its richest glow, and declaring, at the close of every summer day, the time I am losing will never come again? Stung to the heart with this reflection, I started up and mechanically walked to the window. A sweet August morning was smiling without. The dew was not yet dried off the field, the early shadows were stretching cool and dim from the haystacks and the roots of the grand old oaks and thorns scattered along the sunk fence. All was still except the murmur of the scribes about me over their task. I flung up the sash, an uncertain sound of inexpressible sweetness came on a dying gale from the south. I looked in that direction. Huddersfield and the hills beyond it were all veiled in a blue mist, the woods of Hopton and Heaton Lodge were clouding the water's edge, the Calder, silent but bright, was shooting among them like a silver arrow. I listened – the sound sailed full and liquid down the descent: it was the bells of Huddersfield Parish Church. I shut the window and went back to my seat. Then came on me, rushing impetuously, all the mighty phantasm that this had conjured from nothing – from nothing to a system as strange as some religious creed. I felt I could have written gloriously...if I had time to indulge it I felt that the vague suggestions of that moment would have settled down into some narrative better at least than anything I ever produced before. But just then a dolt came up with a lesson. I thought I should have vomited."

Southey was right. Charlotte's romantic stream of consciousness made real life nauseous. For periods she managed to contain her frustrations, telling herself that duty must always come before ambition. She found inspiration in the unmarried Margaret Wooler. For Charlotte, the headmistress would not only become a lifelong friend, but she was proof it was possible to be both single and happy. Knowing the kind of romances she had written about were unlikely ever to become a reality, Charlotte decided to concentrate on the more achievable dream of securing financial independence. The stories of Angria were put away, her passionate ideas of true love were, at least temporarily, shelved and Charlotte became the one thing she had dreaded most – a governess. She had spent many years trying to delay the inevitable, but when her spell at Roe Head came to an end, she admitted defeat and gave in to necessity. A few weeks after her twenty-third birthday she accepted a position as tutor to the children of John Benson Sidgwick in the small village of Lothersdale, near Skipton. It was with a heavy heart with which she left behind her brother, her sisters and she tried desperately to muster some enthusiasm.

Charlotte had long known that work as a governess was the only likely career for a woman of her means, but before she even walked through the door of the Sidgwick family home she was already determined to hate it. While the estate with its gentle stream and clusters of trees was picturesque, Charlotte found much to complain about. At the parsonage the strict hierarchy of class which governed the rest of British society had never intruded. Now for the first time she was made acutely aware of her lot and she didn't like it.

Mrs Sidgwick paid little attention to her children's new governess. She had no reason to, but her disinterest was seen by Charlotte as contempt and she quickly cast her as a woman who had

Within the space of that afternoon he had become convinced that quite by chance he had found a woman with whom he could quite happily spend the rest of his life.

All of which came as something of a surprise to Charlotte. A few days after the visit and four months after Henry's proposal, she received a letter, addressed in an unknown hand. As she opened it, Charlotte wondered what stranger could have cause to write to her. The identity of the author came as something of a shock, but the content of the letter was even more startling. An offer of marriage from a man she had met just once? Some would have been quietly flattered, others might have been carried away on the whirlwind. For Charlotte it was simply ridiculous.

"Well thought I – I've heard of love at first sight but this beats all," she wrote to Ellen after quickly replying to the curate to tell him that sadly she would not be able to accept his offer of becoming Mrs Bryce. "I leave you to guess what my answer would be – convinced that you will not do me the injustice of guessing wrong… I hope you are laughing heartily. This is not like one of my adventures is it?" David Bryce died six months later of a ruptured blood vessel, but the brief moment he touched Charlotte's life further tainted her view of her own chances of marital happiness. She might be the kind of woman tossed a proposal by a well-meaning but misguided curate, but she was now convinced she would never attract a husband who valued her as an equal and who loved her with a fiery passion the years would never quash. Those kind of happy endings didn't happen to someone like her. She wasn't the kind of woman who turned heads as she walked down the street or whom men whispered about in drawing rooms. While she had grown up craving the excitement of some great romance, she now told herself such daydreams would have to come to an end.

Having rejected two marriage proposals because they did not live up to her ideals, and with no likelihood of a third, the only option left was to find another position as a governess. "Duty-Necessity," as she once told Ellen. "These are stern mistresses who will not be disobeyed." It was to be a recurring theme throughout her life.

A governess position soon became available with the White family in Rawdon. They appeared at least on the surface to be a great deal friendlier than the Sidgwicks. The pay was still poor, but Charlotte made a concerted effort to please her new employers. Her subservience lasted just a few months.

"No one but myself is aware how utterly averse my whole mind and nature are to the employment," she complained to the ever-patient Ellen, who by now had become used to the constant and steady stream of her friend's trials and tribulations. "Do not think that I fail to blame myself for this... I find it so hard to repel the rude familiarity of children. I find it so difficult to ask either servants or mistress for anything I want, however much I want it. It is less pain to me to endure the greatest inconvenience than request its removal. Heaven knows I cannot help it I am a fool."

Away from the parsonage Charlotte found it almost impossible to make friends. Whenever she had felt isolated and lonely, she had turned to her fictional world for comfort, but now she found there was little time to indulge her imagination. After the daily lessons with the children, there was needlework to be completed and by the time she earned her freedom it was often after midnight. Homesick for the smell of Tabby baking bread and the sound of Emily playing some new tune she had learnt on the piano, Charlotte became gripped by homesickness. Having persuaded the Whites to

As a child, Charlotte spent many happy hours wandering on the moors above Haworth. Forced to become a governess, she became homesick for the landscape she loved and the freedom it represented.

allow her three weeks off in the summer, the Brontë sisters were reunited and Charlotte was determined they would not be separated again. The plan at first was vague, but was fleshed out during the holidays, largely by Charlotte. By the time she was due to return to the Whites it was settled – the three of them would start their own school. If Charlotte was going to be forced to become a teacher, at least she would be a teacher in charge of her own destiny. Her own situation had been brought into sharp relief by news from Mary. Charlotte's schoolfriend had gone travelling with her brother to France. Her sister had moved to a boarding school in Brussels and her letters spoke of a world of possibility and excitement.

Charlotte read of their exploits, the interesting people they had met, the cities they had visited and the architecture which seemed a world away from the soot-cloaked homes and factories of West Yorkshire.

"Mary's letters spoke of some of the pictures and cathedrals she had seen – pictures the most exquisite – and cathedrals the most venerable – I hardly know what swelled to my throat as I read her letter: such a vehement impatience of restraint and steady work," Charlotte told Ellen. "Such a strong wish for wings – wings such as wealth can furnish – such an urgent thirst to see – to know – to learn – something internal seemed to expand boldly for a minute – I was tantalised with the consciousness of faculties unexercised – then all collapsed and I despaired…I know my place is a favourable one for a Governess – what dismays and haunts me sometimes is a conviction that I have no knack for my vocation – if teaching only were requisite it would be smooth and easy – but it is the living in other people's houses – the estrangement from one's real character – the adoption of a cold and frigid apathetic exterior that is painful."

Charlotte's thirst for adventure had been reawakened and this time she wasn't content to confine it to the pages of some book. Her prayers were soon answered.

Hearing of Charlotte's plans, Margaret Wooler offered the sisters the chance of reviving a school at Dewsbury Moor and Aunt Branwell agreed to an initial loan on the basis that no money should be risked before they had pupils in place. However, after a little further investigation it became clear that if the scheme was to be a success Charlotte and her sisters would need to broaden their horizons. They would need at the very least a basic knowledge of French and German. What better way to improve their skills than on the Continent?

"I feel an absolute conviction, that if this advantage were allowed us, it would be the making of us for life," Charlotte wrote to her aunt asking if it were possible to have an advance on the promised money to fund the trip. "Papa will perhaps think it a wild and ambitious scheme; but who ever rose in the world without ambition. When he left Ireland to go to Cambridge University, he was as ambitious as I am now. I want us all to go on. I know we have talents and I want them to be turned to account."

It was agreed. Anne, who was already working as a teacher at Roe Head, would stay on in Yorkshire, while Charlotte and Emily would head across the Channel. There was much to organise. A suitable school had to be chosen, one with a good reputation, but which was within their modest means, travel had to be arranged and the two sisters had to decide what few possessions they were going to take with them. The Pensionnat Heger in Brussels came recommended and during that winter as a flurry of letters passed between Haworth and Belgium, Charlotte, now twenty-five-years-old, had much cause to pinch herself. Here finally was the chance for the freedom she had so long craved. Christmas that year arrived with much more excitement than usual and when the New Year came, Charlotte's plans were finalised. She and Emily would start the next chapter of their lives that February and while she didn't know it yet, in Brussels her all consuming passion would finally find a target. Hundreds of miles away from the places and people she had grown up with, Charlotte's romantic childhood dreams would be reignited. They would not be extinguished until June 29, 1854, when after three proposals and two passionate affairs, she walked into her father's church in Haworth and of her own free will married a man she didn't love.

2. Heart Inflamed and Broken

"Of all the pains, the greatest pain
Is to love, and love in vain."
George Granville

Charlotte had a thirst for new experiences and the uncomfortable eleven-hour journey from Leeds to London did little to quench it. Patrick had insisted on accompanying his two daughters to Brussels. The harsh winter had taken its toll on his parishioners, leaving many desperate for both financial and spiritual support, but it was his children who needed him most now.

Endless paperwork still needed to be completed before they could set sail and as Patrick busied himself filling out the various forms, it gave the sisters ample opportunity to explore the capital. Charlotte had planned their itinerary with all the detail of a military operation. Nothing was to be left to chance. Determined to see for herself what she had only previously read about in books, once one attraction had been explored, it was onto the next. For Charlotte's old school friend, Mary Tayor, who having previously visited Brussels had agreed to travel with the family, it wasn't the leisurely start to the trip she had imagined.

"She seemed to think our business was, and ought to be, to see all the pictures and statues we could," Mary later remembered. "She knew the artists and knew where other productions of theirs were to be found. I don't remember what we saw except St Paul's."

Charlotte remembered everything. From her room in the Chapter Coffee House in Paternoster Row she could see the great dome of the cathedral and hear the bells toll for morning service. She may never have been to London before, but using the capital's famous landmarks as signposts she led the small party through its streets. As she did the weariness which had cast a shadow over the previous few years was replaced by a new found enthusiasm for life. While her father was making the necessary arrangements with the Belgian consul, Charlotte was being overawed by Westminster Abbey and the National Gallery. Around every corner was some new sight and each was more impressive than the last. Mary may have despaired as her friend hurried them from the British Museum to the Houses of Parliament with barely time to draw breath in between, but Charlotte was too busy to notice her raised eyebrows or hear her tired sighs. She knew every inch of Haworth and had grown bored of walking its streets. In London, Charlotte was happy to be a stranger, happy to be able to discover things for the first time and happy to not quite know what each new day might bring. She had been given the opportunity to taste another life and she wasn't about to waste it.

Those three days in London gave Charlotte a brief, but exhausting glimpse into a world of possibilities. She watched important looking men hurrying to clinch some new business deal, she saw beautiful women in the kind of fine dresses she was sure she would never have occasion to wear and she overheard snatches of conversations about lives which sounded far more exciting than her own. As she queued with her sister and father along the banks of the River Thames waiting to board the small steamship which would take them to Ostend, Charlotte had cause to reflect just how much had changed in a few short months. After bemoaning the "monotonous course" her life had so far run, her wish had been granted. She may have been swapping one classroom for another, but for one whole year she would be living in what she would later describe as the "wide dreamland of Europe" and when she returned she would hopefully have taken charge of her own destiny. Charlotte knew little about the school to which she and Emily were heading and even less about Brussels itself, but as she stared out across the vast blue expanse of water, Charlotte's expectations became increasingly inflated. She was going into the unknown, but anything had to be an improvement on what she was leaving behind. After fourteen hours of sailing, the Brontë party arrived in Belgium and began the final leg of their journey. They were all tired, but for Charlotte the promise of better things made even the ordinary seem spectacular; sleep could wait.

Compared to the dramatic scenery of her home town, where the colours of the moors could change in an afternoon and where the weather of all four seasons often came in one day, the Belgian countryside was unremarkable, boring even. However, as Charlotte gazed out of the window of the stagecoach, which slowly carried them the seventy or so miles to Brussels, she viewed what lay before her with uncritical eyes.

She would later recount those first impressions in the pages of *The Professor* and while the description may have enjoyed the added gloss of fiction there is little doubt the sentiments were all Charlotte's own.

"This is Belgium, reader — look!" says the narrator William Crimsworth, his words full of the same intensity of emotion with which their author had begun this new exciting chapter of her life. "Don't call the picture a flat or a dull one — it was neither flat nor dull to me when I first beheld it. When I left Ostend on a mild February morning and found myself on the road to Brussels, nothing could look vapid to me. My sense of enjoyment possessed an edge whetted to the finest, untouched, keen, exquisite…I gazed often and always with delight from the window of diligence…Well! and what did I see? I will tell you faithfully. Green, reedy swamps, fields fertile but flat, cultivated in patches that made them look like magnified kitchen gardens; belts of cut trees, formal as pollard windows, skirting the horizon; narrow canals, gliding slow by the roadside, painted Flemish farm-houses some very dirty hovels, a grey dead sky, wet roads, wet fields, wet house-tops; not a beautiful, scarcely a picturesque object met my eye along the whole route, yet to me, all was beautiful, all was more than picturesque."

Had Charlotte looked out that morning and seen slums and workhouses she would have no doubt found something good to say about them. Brussels had become the embodiment of all her many years of daydreaming. It was her escape route and her entire future happiness depended on making it a success. By the time the stagecoach had made its way into the city centre night had fallen and it wasn't until early the next morning that Charlotte got a chance to explore. Brussels had been enjoying a decade long period of expansion, new city districts had been added, the demolition of the old city walls had begun and it would soon try to rival Paris as a centre of arts and culture. The Pensionnat Heger in the city's historic quarter had come recommended by Evan Jenkins, chaplain at the

It was an unremarkable building in an unremarkable street, but within the Pensionnat Heger Charlotte embarked on the most extraordinary journey of her life. (courtesy of the Brontë Society)

British embassy in Brussels, who had stressed the honest hardworking reputation of its head Madame Claire Zoe Heger. Charlotte already felt sure she would like her. Worried about extra hidden costs of lessons and materials, she had written to Madame Heger before she and Emily had left England carefully outlining the details of their modest budget. Her response had been both reassuring and understanding and Charlotte was eager to meet her face to face. Patrick was also keen to see whether the school was a suitable place to leave his two single daughters. Neither was disappointed.

Nestled in a row of 17th century properties on a narrow street and just a few minutes walk from the main public park, the school wasn't grand, but it was well kept and Patrick noted that those they passed along the way looked a good deal healthier than the average resident of Haworth.

Having welcomed her two new students, Madame Heger gave Charlotte and Emily a tour of the two light and airy schoolrooms. She showed them the large dormitory where they would sleep with the other girls and pointed them to a section which had been separated by a curtain to give them a little more privacy. Finally she took them out to the garden, a place she said they could find a moment of quiet solace when lessons were finished. Backing onto a walkway which linked Pensionnat Heger with the local boys' school, the garden and its small orchard was the source of much classroom gossip. Fearing the mere sight of a boy may distract her girls from the very serious business of conjugating verbs, Madame Heger had declared a small area of the garden strictly off-limits. Anyone wanting to pursue their amorous intentions would have had to fight through the tangled ivy and overgrown jasmine bushes, but with forbidden fruits always the most sought after many of the girls spent much of their spare time desperately trying to peer through the thorns in the hope of glimpsing just what it was their dignity was being protected from.

Such schoolgirl indulgences didn't concern Charlotte. She had not come to Brussels to giggle about what temptations may lay beyond the shrubbery; she and Emily had come to learn. While the other pupils had to be constantly reminded about the importance of punctuality and private study, Charlotte was so consumed by her lessons that it was some months before she found the time to write to Ellen her friend back home. When she finally did put pen to paper, the excitement with which she had left Haworth was undiminished.

"I am a schoolgirl, a complete schoolgirl and, on the whole very happy in that capacity," she wrote, clearly enjoying having thrown off the weary responsibility of being a governess. "It felt very strange at first to submit to authority instead of exercising it – to obey orders instead of giving them; but I like that state of things. I returned to it with the same avidity that a cow, that has long been kept on dry hay returns to fresh grass. Don't laugh at my simile. It is natural to me to submit and very unnatural to command."

Desperate to learn, Charlotte relished being back in the classroom, but the optimism which had carried her across the Channel didn't last. In its place the all too familiar feelings of loneliness and frustration returned.

Charlotte was considerably older than the rest of the pupils who she concluded were frivolously immature. She was a Protestant, they without exception were Roman Catholic, a religion she had always thought vastly inferior to her own. Having arrived with only a little knowledge of French, Charlotte struggled in the early days to

Constantin Heger was 59-years-old when this portrait was painted. Charlotte always remembered him as the young, passionate teacher.

understand the informal conversations going on around her. By the time her vocabulary expanded, it didn't matter, she had already decided there was no one she wished to be friends with.

"If the national character of the Belgians is to be measured by the character of most of the girls in the school," she wrote again to Ellen just a few weeks after her first letter. "It is a character singularly cold, selfish, animal and inferior."

Neither Charlotte nor Emily made any attempt to fit in. They had each other, they had their books and that, they told themselves, was enough. If they were "isolated in the midst of numbers" as Charlotte suggested it was largely their own fault. Even those who did extend the hand of friendship soon learnt not to bother.

Knowing the sisters were alone in a foreign country, Mr Jenkins and his wife regularly invited them to spend Sundays with them and their two sons. Not wanting to appear rude, Charlotte and Emily often accepted, but both looked liked they would rather be anywhere else. The afternoons were littered with uncomfortable silences and stilted conversations that went nowhere and to the relief of all concerned the invites soon stopped arriving.

Just as they had been back home in Haworth, the sisters were self-sufficient for conversation and entertainment. While their shyness was often mistaken for aloofness, Charlotte had never cared much for the opinion of outsiders.

However, what she didn't know was there was someone close by whose thoughts and feelings she would come to value more than anyone else's. For the first time in her life Charlotte was about to meet a man who appeared to care about brains not beauty, who read as avidly as she did and who would show her how to channel her imagination into more structured flowing prose.

When not teaching French and maths at the nearby boys' school, Constantin Heger instructed his wife's pupils in the art of literature. He was 35-years-old, a natural teacher, who was quick to spot talent and who was unconcerned if it came at the expense of polite conversation and easy pleasantries. He would prove to be everything Charlotte wanted most in life, but it was far from love at first sight. Monsieur Heger may have been both intelligent and incisive, but he was also deeply serious. He could reduce his pupils to tears by a single well-placed glance over his wire-rimmed spectacles and while he commanded great respect, he demanded much from his students. As Charlotte's less than flattering summary put it, he was an odd looking man with a temperament to suit.

"There is one individual of whom I have not yet spoken," she told Ellen that summer. "M. Heger, the husband of Madame. He is a professor of rhetoric, a man of power as to mind, but very choleric and irritable as to temperament; a little black ugly being with a face that varies in expression. Sometimes he borrows the lineaments of an insane tom-cat, sometimes those of a delirious hyena, but very seldom he discards these perilous attractions and assumes an air not above 100 degrees removed from mild and gentlemanlike. He is very angry with me just at present, because I have written a translation which he chose to stigmatise as peu correct. He did not tell me so, but wrote the accusation on the margin of my book and asked in brief, stern phrase, how it happened that my compositions were always better than my translations? Adding that the thing seemed to him inexplicable. The fact is, some weeks ago, in a high-flown humour, he forbade me to use either dictionary or grammar in translating the most difficult English passages into French. This makes the task rather arduous, and compels me now and then to introduce an English word, which nearly plucks the eyes out of his head when he sees it…when he is very ferocious with me I cry; that sets all things straight…The few private lessons M Heger has vouchsafed to give us are, I suppose, to be considered a great favour, and I can perceive they have already excited much spite and jealousy in the school."

If the description of Monsieur Heger bore more than a little resemblance to Charlotte's later fictional creations of Mr Rochester and Paul Emanuel, it was with good reason. By the end of her stay in Brussels, the romantic leads of Angria would finally be laid to rest, replaced by men who thought much more than they acted and whose bravery didn't lie on the battlefield but in tearing up the rulebook by which the rest of society was governed. These were heroes prepared to become social outcasts for love and who much preferred a finely tuned mind to a pretty face.

Monsieur Heger was certainly quick to see the potential in his two new English pupils and unlike many of those who passed through his classroom he was sure their money had not been wasted. He may have been a disciplinarian, banning the use of dictionaries and grammar books on which he felt his students were too reliant, but he was also dedicated to awakening a desire to learn. He burned with the kind of inspiration Charlotte herself had been incapable of mustering in her own pupils and she came to thrive on it. Many of their lessons were spent analysing passages from classic French literature. Once every sentence had been dissected, Monsieur Heger would order them to write a response similar in style to the original. To both Charlotte and Emily such a workmanlike approach to the business of words was an anathema. They had always written exactly what they thought when they thought it. Emotion took priority over

itself in the grip of industrial unrest. Riots had broken out across Yorkshire and many of Patrick's parishioners had been left fearing for both their safety and their jobs. Against this backdrop of uncertainty, the shadow of death once again fell over the parsonage.

William Weightman had arrived in Haworth three years earlier as Patrick's clerical assistant. While dedicated to his work, he had never felt it necessary to prove his religious fervour with sombre looks. Always a light-hearted presence in the parsonage, he had made it his business to flirt with the young Brontë sisters. He had once walked ten miles to send them Valentine's cards and both Charlotte and her younger sister Anne had been more than a little flattered by his efforts. However, an amiable character was no defence against disease. As the summer passed into autumn, William, a regular visitor to the sick and poverty stricken, became one of the many thousands to be struck down that year by cholera. Branwell had been a constant presence by his friend's bedside, but there was nothing which could be done. He died that autumn at the age of twenty-eight. It was a bitter blow for Patrick, who had treated William more like a son than a colleague, but there was little time for reflection. Just a few days later the woman who without a second thought had moved from her home hundreds of miles away in Cornwall to look after her sister's children fell ill. Aunt Branwell had always been robust, easily shirking off coughs and colds, but writhing in agony her stomach in spasms, it quickly became clear this was one time she wouldn't bounce back.

By the time the letter informing Charlotte of her aunt's death arrived, the funeral had already taken place and she had also just heard that Martha Taylor, the younger sister of her friend Mary, had also died. It may have been too late to pay her formal respects, but with the lives of three of her closest friends and family snuffed out within a matter of weeks of each other, Charlotte felt the need to go home. It was nine months since she had last seen Haworth and even though it meant leaving behind the man she was fast falling in love with, she knew she could only begin to make sense of all the recent bad news surrounded by familiar sights and sounds.

Emily, who had never settled at the school, was more than happy to leave Brussels. As they packed their belongings and arranged their tickets, Charlotte had less time than usual to think about Monsieur Heger, but she was sure that this would only be a temporary separation. There was still so much she had to learn and the letter he wrote to her father was confirmation she would see him again soon.

In truth it was little more than a school report and an assurance that once matters had been sorted at home, he would be more than happy for the sisters to return to finish their studies. However, to Charlotte it was sign that Monsieur Heger saw her as more than just a diligent pupil.

"I have not the honour of knowing you personally and yet I have profound admiration for you," he wrote to Patrick. "For in judging the father of a family by his children one cannot be mistaken and in this respect the education and sentiments that we have found in your daughters can only give us a very high idea of your worth and of your character." Charlotte's heart swelled with pride as she saw sentiments Monsieur Heger himself had never intended: "You will undoubtedly learn with pleasure that your children have made extraordinary progress in all the branches of learning and that this progress is entirely due to their love of work and their perseverance. With pupils like this we had very little to do; their progress is more your work than ours. We did not have to teach them the value of time and instruction; they had learnt all this in their paternal home and we have only had on our part the slight merit of directing their efforts and providing suitable material for the praiseworthy activity which your daughters have drawn from your examples and your lessons. You must believe, sir, this is not a question of personal interest with us, it is a question of affection. You will pardon me if we speak of your children, if we interest ourselves in their welfare, as if they were part of our own family; their personal qualities, their good will, their extreme zeal are the only reason which compel us to risk your displeasure."

When Charlotte arrived back home with Emily in early November the dark nights had already closed in around the parsonage. It was good to see her father again, but there was unfinished business in Brussels and she made it clear that she planned to return after Christmas. Charlotte had suspected she might have to make the return journey alone and she was right. The death of their aunt had unexpectedly given Emily the chance to roam the moors and she wasn't going to give up her one main pleasure in life so easily again. She told the rest of the family that her father needed her at home, but they all knew the real reason for her reluctance to go back to Brussels. The only place Emily was ever truly happy was at home. At the Pensionnat Heger she may have been able to improve her French and German, but it was no compensation for the wild landscape she loved so much. In contrast, Charlotte couldn't wait to leave. To her, the holidays seemed to never end. However, after many sleepless nights spent dreaming of the man she had left behind in Belgium, Charlotte began to retrace her steps.

Travelling alone to London was not without risk and when she

Following the death of her father's curate and her aunt, Charlotte needed to be surrounded by the comforting familiarity of home. However, it was not long before her thoughts turned back to Brussels and Monsieur Heger.

arrived late at night she found herself on the rain and windswept dockside trying desperately to find the boat she was booked on.

It was pitch black and bitterly cold and all Charlotte could hear was the sound of the dockworkers whose language would have made her own father blush.

After what seemed like hours, but which was probably just minutes, Charlotte found her boat. Exhausted, she struggled with her heavy trunk, but was told no passengers were allowed to sleep on board. On the verge of tears Charlotte asked to speak to someone in charge. Thankfully, the captain was not the kind to force a young woman to spend a night on the river when a perfectly good cabin lay empty indoors and he ushered her on board.

She fell quickly to sleep and when she woke early the next morning to see the boat pushing on towards Belgium, the stresses of the previous night were forgotten. She didn't think of the watermen she had tipped far too much or the coachman who had driven off as soon as he had got his money. Instead she closed her eyes and thought of Monsieur Heger.

Having agreed to take on some teaching duties while continuing her own studies, when Charlotte arrived back at the school she was told she could now use the family's sitting room whenever she pleased. It wasn't a place she felt particularly comfortable and she had no desire to watch Monsieur Heger play out his roles as both a father and a husband. The moments she craved were those when they were alone, moments when she was the only focus of his attention. Much to her delight she soon found they would now have more time together than ever before.

Desperate to improve his English pronunciation and perfect his turn of phrase, Monsieur Heger asked Charlotte if she would give him some private tuition. His brother-in-law also sat in on the lessons, but he couldn't have helped but notice that he wasn't the teacher's favourite.

Charlotte delighted in being able to share with the man who had already taught her so much a little of her own knowledge. They were some of the happiest hours she spent in Brussels. Occasionally when she turned to the blackboard she couldn't help smiling at how their positions had been reversed and nothing made her laugh more than when Monsieur Heger's beautiful French lilt was mangled into the strange sounds as he tried and failed to imitate her own accent.

Charlotte rarely had cause to venture outside of the school grounds, but when Easter arrived, Brussels woke up from its winter slumber and its streets and squares were alive with entertainment. For a few weeks the town hall with its gothic tower and the medley of guild buildings which framed the market square were no longer the city's commercial heart, but a theatrical backdrop for dancers and musicians.

The annual carnival was always a highpoint of the calendar and Monsieur Heger was keen to make sure his brightest student didn't miss out. He also took another pupil on the trip, but Charlotte was sure it was she who had been singled out for special attention. In parts they had to fight their way through the crowds and Charlotte often struggled to see what was going on. She didn't care. All that mattered was that they were together and the more time she spent in his company the more she felt sorry for those who didn't have their own Monsieur Heger close at hand.

"She has no one to be as good to her as M. Heger is to me; to lend her books to converse with her etc," she wrote to Ellen after receiving a letter from Mary who was not bearing the death of her

invited Charlotte into her home, gone out of her way to fit her timetable around the Brontë's budget and invited her back as a teacher. In return Charlotte had fallen for her husband. However, it wasn't Madame Heger who had changed, it was Charlotte.

Had she been able to step back and view the scene impartially, she would have realised that every injustice she accused Madame Heger of, could quite easily have been laid at the door of her husband. However, to accuse him of trampling on her feelings and neglecting her in a time of crisis, would have been to admit that she had been wrong, that Monsieur Heger had only ever regarded her as another pupil, albeit a talented one.

Charlotte may have grown up with an acute sense of right and wrong, but now the line became blurred. Unwilling to confront the fact that the man she wanted to share her innermost hopes and dreams was already happily married, she convinced herself she was the woman wronged.

Writing somewhat cryptically to Ellen, she implied Madame Heger was not quite the good character everyone assumed her to be and   promised to tell her more when she herself was certain of the facts. Her secrecy was unnecessary. Rumours Charlotte had returned to Brussels with some motive other than completing her studies were already circulating at home.

"Three or four people it seems have the idea that the future epoux of Mademoiselle Brontë is on the Continent." Even in denying the depths of her feelings to Ellen she couldn't resist a little French flourish. "These people are wiser than I am – they could not believe that I crossed the sea merely to return as teacher to Mde Heger…I must forsooth have some remote hope of entrapping a husband somehow – or somewhere – If these charitable people knew the total seclusion of the life I lead – that I never exchange a word with any other man than Monsieur Heger and seldom indeed with him they would perhaps cease to suppose that any such chimerical and groundless notion influenced my proceedings. Have I said enough to clear myself of so silly an imputation? Not that it is a crime to marry, or a crime to wish to be married; but it is an imbecility which I reject with contempt for women who have neither fortune or beauty to make marriage the principle object of their wishes and hopes and the aim of all their actions…not to be able to convince themselves they are unattractive and that they had better be quiet and think of other things than wedlock."

The lady, Ellen must have thought as she read Charlotte's letter that April, did protest just a little too much. Charlotte tried to convince herself that anything broaching a relationship with Monsieur Heger, who was about to become father to a fifth child, was an impossibility, but it was pointless. The loud beating of her heart drowned out the commonsense advice of her head.

"The fact is I have far keener feelings than any other human being I ever knew," she had written some years before and now that same torrid stream of emotions threatened to overwhelm her.

Growing up, Charlotte had filled any moment of quiet with harmless daydreams, now feeling more isolated than ever her imagination sent her on a dangerous path towards heartbreak and emotional collapse.

The holidays, when most of the pupils went home and an eerie silence fell on the school, had never been a particularly happy time for Charlotte. As the summer approached and as five long lonely weeks stretched out before her, she knew she had to keep herself occupied. In an attempt to escape the oppressive atmosphere of the

Charlotte had little time for the Catholic faith, but as the pressure of her aching heart grew and with no one to confide in, she entered the Catholic cathedral in Brussels and confessed her sins to a priest. (courtesy of the Brontë Society)

school and clear her head, Charlotte took to walking the streets. Each day she would spend hours wandering around Brussels, sitting down by the river and watching the tradesmen go about their business, but it was no good. Charlotte took her claustrophobia with her and wherever she went thoughts of Monsieur Heger were always at the forefront of her mind. Usually on these trips she saw much, but registered little. Her only aim was to keep on walking until she knew the light was fading and she could return to the school and slip quietly into bed. However, one day that August she felt drawn to the city's Catholic cathedral. She had seen the church a dozen times before and until that day she had never felt any compulsion to see beyond its gothic façade. Charlotte crossed the small park nearby, walked up the flight of stone steps and once inside joined those waiting to confess their sins. When she later related the incident to Emily, it was done in the same kind of tone she might have used to tell her about buying a new bonnet. However, while Charlotte played down its significance, to those who knew her it was further sign of a deeply troubled mind. A Protestant who had little regard for Catholicism, Charlotte had made no secret of her dislike for religious pomp and ceremony. However, now the woman who usually went out of her way to avoid new and awkward situations, knelt down on the altar steps and despite having no idea of the correct words or the prayers she was supposed to recite, through a grate she confessed her sins.

"After I had watched two or three penitents go and return, I approached at last and knelt down in a niche which was just vacated…It was a funny position. I felt exactly as I did when alone on the Thames at midnight…but I was determined to confess and at last he said he would allow me because it might be the first step towards returning to the true church. I actually did confess – a real confession. When I had done he told me his address and said that every morning I was to go to his house and he would reason with me and try to convince me of the error and enormity of being a Protestant!!! I promised faithfully to go. Of course, however, the adventure stops there, and I hope I shall never see the priest again. I think you had better not tell papa of this. He will not understand that it was only a freak and will perhaps think I am going to turn Catholic."

Charlotte never confided in anyone what passed between her and the priest that day, she didn't need to. The emotional pressure was building and as the cracks grew bigger, she was willing to look for crumbs of comfort in even the most unlikely of places. Unfortunately, the sense of relief she found that day quickly evaporated. Sensing all was not well, her old school friend Mary urged Charlotte to leave Brussels immediately and even offered to share her own teaching job until she found something more suitable. Charlotte declined, but she knew Mary was right. Her world was falling apart and in Brussels she couldn't think straight. Charlotte's thoughts turned once again to Haworth and the simple life she had once known. She desperately wanted to be back in the kitchen watching Tabby make dinner and hearing Emily telling her to make sure she kept enough meat back to feed Keeper, the family's large mastiff. She even missed her boiled potatoes which were without fail always overcooked.

If Charlotte could have left that minute, she would, but she still feared being seen as a failure. Slumping into a depression, the letters she wrote to family and friends struck an increasingly desperate note. As the leaves began to turn brown and the nights became shorter, Charlotte hoped Emily might take it upon herself to tell her father of her obvious distress and that very soon a letter would arrive telling her to trouble herself no more and ordering her to come back home immediately. The letter never came and Charlotte, forced to take matters into her own hands, half-heartedly handed in her resignation. She expected it to be eagerly accepted, but Madame Heger had more compassion than Charlotte had ever given credit for and she did not want to lose a talented teacher. The next day she was summoned by Monsieur Heger, who "pronounced with vehemence his decision" that she should stay, an intervention which served only to further fan the flames of her destructive passion. Charlotte was unable to keep her mind on her studies. Realising she had not written anything for months and in the hope of restoring her interest in the school, Monsieur Heger took it upon himself to fill the large gaps in her knowledge of mathematics. It was not a subject for which Charlotte had any particular love and the same challenging teaching technique which had won her over in literature, now just made her frustrated and she soon gave up. On the brink of nervous collapse, Charlotte knew that she had to leave and this time nobody, not even Monsieur Heger, could persuade her otherwise.

There was no farewell party. Charlotte had made few friends and there was only one person she was going to miss. As she said goodbye, Monsieur Heger handed her a diploma certificate. It was the reason she had left home in the first place, but in Brussels she had found more than a knowledge of French and German. Charlotte boarded the stagecoach out of the city on December 31, but there was little of the hope and expectation which usually heralds the New Year.

By the time she walked through the doors of the parsonage she

letter to tell her he had been thinking about her and that he missed her just a fraction as much as she pined for him.

Each day she waited for the post, but each day she was disappointed.

Her anguish grew ever greater, until she could bear it no more.

"I am told that you are working too hard and that your health has suffered somewhat in consequence," she wrote in a letter she hoped would prick his conscience. "For that reason I refrain from uttering a single complaint for your long silence – I would rather wait six months without receiving news from you than add one grain to the weight, already too heavy, which overwhelms you.

"Ah, Monsieur! I once wrote you a letter that was less than reasonable, because sorrow was at my heart; but I shall do so no more – I shall try to be selfish no longer; and even while I look upon your letters as one of the greatest felicities known to me I shall await the receipt of them in patience until it pleases you and suits you to send me any…I greatly fear that I shall forget French, for I am firmly convinced that I shall see you again some day – I know not how or when – but it must be, for I wish it so much, and then I should not wish to remain dumb before you – it would be too sad to see you and not be able to speak to you. To avoid such misfortune I learn every day by heart half a page of French from a book written in familiar style: and I take pleasure in learning this lesson, Monsieur; as I pronounce the French words it seems to me as if I were chatting with you."

Charlotte signed it 'Your Grateful Pupil' but it would have been obvious to anyone, not least Madame Heger, that she wanted an entirely different relationship. Charlotte's feelings were there in black and white and with Monsieur Heger perhaps rightly concluding that any response would be seen as justification for her feelings, the letter, like many others, went unanswered.

Charlotte was in limbo. She couldn't forget the past and she couldn't bear to think of a future without Monsieur Heger in it. When Emily asked why she didn't write poetry anymore, she told her like their father she feared she was going blind. Her sister was too kind to point out her failing eyesight hadn't stopped the long screeds to Brussels in which she told Monsieur Heger should she ever manage to write again, her first book would be dedicated to him.

Her memory of him would in fact inspire entire novels, but nothing she said moved him to respond and the letters she wrote to him were torn up destined never to be read by anyone else. It is not known who later pieced them back together, but what is certain is that what had started out as a schoolgirl crush had now turned into a dangerous obsession.

"For six months I have been waiting for a letter from Monsieur — six months' waiting is very long, you know," she wrote again, the tone increasing in desperation with every letter. "However, I do not complain, and I shall be richly rewarded for a little sorrow if you will now write a letter…I shall be satisfied with the letter however brief it be – only do not forget to tell me of your health Monsieur and how Madame and the children are, and the governesses and the pupils…Farewell Monsieur; I am depending on soon having your news. The idea delights me, for the remembrance of your kindness will never fade from my memory and as long as that remembrance endures the respect with which it has inspired me will endure likewise."

In the silence which again followed, Charlotte was left to make

Hundreds of miles away from the man she loved, Charlotte scrawled a series of heartfelt letters and each day prayed her broken heart would be mended by a reply.

excuses on his behalf. He was ill. The duties of the school year were taking their toll. It was exam time. Or, and this was the explanation Charlotte favoured, his wife was preventing him from writing. Even in sleep she couldn't find solace.

"Day and night I find neither rest nor peace," she wrote again. It was a full year since she had left Brussels, but her feelings for Monsieur Heger were undiminished. "If I sleep I am disturbed by tormenting dreams in which I see you, always severe, always grave, always incensed against me. Forgive me then, Monsieur, if I adopt the course of writing to you again. How can I endure life if I make no effort to ease its sufferings? I know that you will be irritated when your read this letter. You will say once more that I am hysterical or neurotic – that I have black thoughts etc. So be it Monsieur; I do not seek to justify myself; I submit to every sort of reproach. All I know is that I cannot, that I will not resign myself to lose wholly the friendship of my master. I would rather suffer the greatest physical pain than always have my heart lacerated from smarting regrets. If my master withdraws his friendship from me entirely I should be altogether without hope; if he gives me a little – just a little – I shall be satisfied – happy; I shall have reason for living on, for working Monsieur, the poor have not need of much to sustain them – they ask only for the crumbs that fall from the rich men's table. But if they are refused the crumbs they die of hunger. Nor do I, either, need much affection from those I love. I should not know what to do with a friendship entire and complete – I am not used to it. But you showed me of yore a little interest – I hold onto it as I would hold onto life.

"You will tell me perhaps – 'I take not the slightest interest in you Mademoiselle Charlotte. You are no longer an inmate of my House;

I have forgotten you'.

"Well, Monsieur, tell me so frankly. It will be a shock to me. It matters not. It would be less dreadful than uncertainty…One suffers in silence so long as he has the strength to do so and when that strength gives out one speaks without too carefully measuring one's words.

"I wish Monsieur happiness and prosperity."

Charlotte posted the letter, but while she felt she had asked for little, she got nothing. Her friend Mary, who had been on one of her many adventures, had written to say she was travelling back to England via Brussels before moving to New Zealand. Charlotte was shocked at the news of her planned immigration, but she couldn't help but see a little silver lining. If Mary was coming back through Belgium, perhaps she would bring with her a letter that perhaps Monsieur Heger hadn't dare trust to the post. Mary arrived empty handed and even the imaginative Charlotte was running out of excuses. She might have told herself that he kept her many letters wrapped in ribbon, hidden away from prying eyes only to be looked at when no one else was around. She might even have convinced herself that he was desperate to reply, but felt to do so would be disloyal to his wife and children. Had she ever known the truth, that on the edge of one of her heartfelt letters, Monsieur Heger had scribbled the name and address of his shoemaker her already delicate heart would have been broken beyond repair.

As Charlotte struggled to make sense of how one man had turned her life completely upside down, she went to visit Ellen. The trip passed pleasantly enough, but when she arrived back home, she found Branwell drunk and jobless.

It emerged he had been sacked from his position as tutor when his employer discovered he was more interested in his wife than his children's education. Lydia Robinson was seventeen years older than Branwell and while flattered by his attentions she wasn't about to sacrifice a comfortable existence for a man who couldn't even support himself. Branwell was much less pragmatic. He had lost the woman he loved and he was not about to bear it quietly. Charlotte, who knew how it felt to be in love with the unobtainable, could feel no pity. Stoically and quietly she had absorbed her hurt, Branwell drank to numb his feelings and when he thought he could feel nothing at all he drank some more just to be sure. As the fall out from the Robinson affair continued, Charlotte's thoughts returned to her own broken heart.

"I tell you frankly that I have tried meanwhile to forget you, for the remembrance of a person whom one thinks never to see again, and for whom, nevertheless, one greatly esteems, frets too much the mind and when one has suffered that kind of anxiety for a year or two, one is ready to do anything to find peace once more," she wrote in one final attempt to make Monsieur Heger realise just how much she depended on him. "I have done everything; I have sought occupations; I have denied myself absolutely the pleasure of speaking about you – even to Emily; but I have been able to conquer neither my regrets nor my impatience. That indeed is humiliating – to be unable to control one's thoughts, to be the slave of a regret, of a memory, the slave of a fixed dominant idea which lords it over the mind. Why cannot I have just as much friendship for you, as you for me – neither more nor less? Then should I be so tranquil, so free – I could keep silence then for ten years without an effort…to write to an old pupil cannot be an interesting occupation for you, I know, but for me it is life. Your last letter was stay and prop to me –

weren't the usual trite musings about love and marriage so many writers were guilty of, they were something much more heartfelt. They talked not of hearts and flowers, but of stirring passion and powerful emotion. It was some time later when Charlotte finally put down Emily's notebook and when she did, she was convinced. The Brontë sisters were to become published authors. It had been something they had talked about before, but never with any real degree of seriousness. Now Charlotte was prepared to pursue the dream with as much fervour as she had Monsieur Heger. She knew no publisher would take a risk on three unknown and unproven poets, but that didn't matter. Aunt Branwell had left them each some money in her will and Charlotte decided they would invest a little of it in her plan. All she had to do next was convince her two sisters. It was no easy task. The cost of publishing even the smallest volume of poetry was the equivalent of three-quarters of a governess's average annual salary. Charlotte, however, was undaunted and if Emily and Anne made any dissenting noises, she chose not to hear them. Two and a half years after she had returned heartbroken from Brussels, the volume, simply entitled *Poems by Currer, Acton and Ellis Bell* arrived at Haworth. The pseudonyms had been decided on by all three sisters. They knew work by a female hand would be judged automatically inferior and they hoped their choice of names might give them a better chance of success. It didn't work. By the end of the year just two copies had been sold. However, by the time they discovered the book was destined to disappear without a trace, the sisters were already on with a new venture. While Charlotte's time in Brussels had ended spectacularly badly, it had also shown her there was life beyond the four walls of the parsonage. Monsieur Heger had proved the biggest disappointment of her life, but he hadn't completely broken her spirit. She still longed, she told Ellen, to "travel, work, to live a life of action." By winning fame as an author she hoped to escape from the funerial atmosphere of home once and for all.

Charlotte had learnt much from the process of publishing the first book, but now decided the recognition she craved did not lie in poetry. Gathering her two sisters around she told them of her new plan. They would, she said, each write a novel. All three would be published, still under their pseudonyms, in the same volume and together they would prove the female hand was as worthy as that of any male. Charlotte immediately began work on *The Professor*. Had she bothered even occasionally to look up from her writing desk she might have noticed the longing glances being shot in her direction from her father's curate. With Patrick still awaiting the cataract operation he hoped might restore his sight, Arthur Bell Nicholls had become an even more frequent visitor to the parsonage than usual. His was almost a constant presence and there was a growing possibility that he might have other things on his mind than simply a sense of duty. Ellen had heard the gossip and couldn't help teasing her friend about Arthur's amorous intentions. Charlotte did not see the funny side. While she had once analysed even the smallest hand gesture of Monsieur Heger, now she was blind to even the most obvious attention. Arthur she insisted was barely a friend, if anything more an acquaintance, and any talk of marriage was quickly stamped out.

"Who gravely asked you whether Miss Brontë was not going to be married to her papa's Curate," she replied to Ellen, in a tone devoid of its usual lightness. "I scarcely need say that never was rumour more unfounded — it puzzles me to think how it could to feel pleasure and if no-one else was going to provide it, she would have to. Returning to Haworth, her father's sight greatly improved, Charlotte's love affair with her heroine continued. For three solid weeks she did nothing but write, the only interruption, the arrival of bailiffs at the front door demanding payment for Branwell's mounting debts.

Charlotte realised that while she had spent years obsessing about a man who had given her little more than a second thought, her own life had been held in suspended animation. The writing of *Jane Eyre* gave her moments of genuine hope for a better future, but all too often they were punctured by the fear she may have already left it too late.

"I know life is passing away and I am doing nothing – earning nothing a very bitter knowledge it is at moments," she wrote to Ellen that autumn. "But I see no way out of the mist. More than one very favourable opportunity has now offered which I have been obliged to put aside, probably when I am free to leave home I shall neither be able to find place nor employment – perhaps too I shall be quite past the prime of my life – my faculties will be rusted – and my few acquirements in great measure forgotten – These ideas sting me keenly – but whenever I consult my Conscience it affirms that I am doing right in staying at home and bitter are its upbraidings when I yield to an eager desire for release."

Charlotte may have only been thirty-years-old, but she felt "grey, sunken and withered". She had wasted years on a man who didn't love her and while she forced herself to finish *Jane Eyre* it was with a slightly heavier heart than she had begun. As winter arrived, Charlotte continued to send out copies of *The Professor*, but as the rejection letters piled up and the house was hit by the usual bout of seasonal coughs and colds there was little light relief. In one last ditched attempt, Charlotte took one of the manuscripts which had been returned to sender, half-heartedly crossed out the address of the original publisher and sent it to Smith, Elder & Co, Cornhill, London. It was not one of the more established publishing houses, but Charlotte was fast running out of options. The response when it came started much the same as all the others. They thanked her for sending the manuscript, but said unfortunately for business reasons it was not the kind of work they were looking to publish. However, this was not the standard rejection Charlotte had become used to receiving and as she read the two-page letter she found a kernel of hope. Recognising she was a writer of some talent, the firm said should she have any other manuscripts they would be more than pleased to take a look. Charlotte reckoned *Jane Eyre* needed a month's work. She finished it in two weeks. The manuscript was sent down to London where it was first read by the firm's talent spotter William Smith Williams. Staying up into the early hours to finish the book, by the end he knew his hunch had been right. He had found a writer of rare genius, someone who could help elevate Smith, Elder & Co above its competitors. The next day he went to see the firm's owner and made him promise to make the book a priority. George Smith had taken over the day-to-day running of the company following the death of his father and was determined to prove he was a worthy successor. He had never seen Smith Williams so animated and was understandably keen to see what the fuss was all about. George worked six days a week at the office and rarely got home before nightfall, but he promised to read the book that Sunday. He picked up the manuscript at breakfast and was instantly captivated. George had arranged to meet a friend that afternoon to scratched out by dim candlelight. He loved it and he wasn't alone. The critics began to deliver their verdicts. One praised its originality, truth and passion, another declared it the best novel of the year and when some dismissed it as coarse, brutal and riddled with unnecessary vice, everyone within London's literary circle suddenly wanted to get their hands on a copy. Charlotte was about to take the literary world by storm.

The first edition quickly sold out and as a second print run was being ordered, talk turned to the real identity of the mysterious Currer Bell. George too couldn't help wondering who had really been responsible for a novel of such passion. He suspected it was probably a woman, but he never once guessed that the hand which created the simmering Mr Rochester and his mad wife Bertha belonged to a parson's daughter who had fallen in love with the wrong man. As word of *Jane Eyre* spread, Emily and Anne's publisher suddenly discovered a renewed interest in their work. Both *Wuthering Heights* and *Agnes Grey* appeared that December. Neither did as well as *Jane Eyre* and when Anne produced her second novel *The Tenant of Wildfell Hall* her publisher, desperate for a little fame of his own, suggested Currer, Ellis and Acton Bell were not three separate authors, but one and the same. Charlotte had no choice. George was clearly concerned by the allegations and if she were to prove to him she hadn't been touting her books to the competition, she and her sisters would have to go and see him in person. Emily, who had prevented Charlotte from telling even her best friend Ellen that she was a published author, was not about to unmask herself to a complete stranger. She refused point blank to be part of the London contingent. Anne was no more inclined, but guilt is a powerful emotion and knowing it was her book which had caused this particular storm, she agreed to travel with her sister. The premises of Smith, Elder & Co were close to the Bank of England in Threadneedle Street and just a short walk from The Monument which had been built to commemorate those who had died in the Great Fire of London and celebrate the rebuilding of the city. On another occasion, Charlotte might have ambled a little, but there was no time to sightsee, they had to get to the publishers as soon as they could.

When they arrived, the shop floor was busy and no one took much notice of the two sisters who were waiting quietly to see George Smith. They had no appointment and wouldn't say what it was that was so urgent, but Charlotte made it clear they had travelled a very long way and they would not leave until they had been seen. It was with some irritation that George broke off from his paperwork to see what two women, who looked little like his usual customers, could possibly want with him.

"I was in the midst of my correspondence, and my thoughts were far away from Currer Bell and *Jane Eyre*," he remembered later. "Two rather quaintly dressed little ladies, pale-faced and anxious-looking, walked into my room…I must confess that my first impression of Charlotte Brontë's personal appearance was that it was interesting rather than attractive. She was very small and had a quaint old fashioned look. Her head seemed too large for her body. She had fine eyes, but her face was marred by the shape of her mouth and by the complexion. There was but little feminine charm about her; and of this fact she was herself uneasily and perpetually conscious. It may seem strange that the possession of genius did not lift her above the weakness of an excessive anxiety about her personal appearance. But I believe she would have given all her genius and her fame to be to their lodgings that afternoon Charlotte felt the onset of a migraine, it was the kind which frequently brought her down just when there was the slightest promise of excitement. Everything had happened in such a rush, she wasn't even sure they had definitely agreed to go to the opera. However, when George arrived a few hours later in full evening dress, complete with white gloves, it became clear he had interpreted their nervous glances as a definite affirmative. With the carriage waiting downstairs, Charlotte and Anne quickly changed. They hadn't brought any fine dresses with them to London, in fact they didn't even own one evening gown between them. Making do with what they had, they stepped into the carriage to see Smith Williams also dressed like a perfect gentleman. Charlotte did wonder how George would explain to his friends what he was doing at the Opera House with two such unfashionably dressed women and she couldn't help smiling as she walked with him up the plush crimson carpet staircase. She knew they looked an unlikely group and she felt sure people were staring, but George seemed not to care, he was after all spending an evening with the much talked about Currer Bell.

The Opera House was an assault on Charlotte's senses. The chandeliers looked like they were dripping in stars, the smell of expensive perfume wafted from every corner and she had never heard so many refined voices in one room before. From start to finish the evening took Charlotte's breath away. It was past one o'clock before she and Anne got to bed and they had to be up early as George, who seemed determined to be their full-time chaperone, had promised to take them to church and then on to his house to dinner.

George amused Charlotte. In his own office he had struck a

confident figure, a man of business much older than his years, but when alone with her he often stumbled over his words. His nervousness was endearing and while she had known him less than twenty-four hours, she had already decided he was both kind and intelligent.

George told Charlotte he had been working at Smith, Elder & Co since he was fourteen-years-old and when his father had died two years previously it had been decided that he was ready to take over. In that short time he had already proved an astute businessman and his mother loved to tell people how very proud she was of her son. In her eyes George could do no wrong and if he wanted to invite two painfully shy women to dinner, she would do her best to make them feel at ease.

Charlotte didn't have much appetite for the food Mrs Smith prepared, but the afternoon in the company of George and his two sisters, who were also blessed with the knack of effortless conversation, passed pleasantly enough. Charlotte, who often found herself rendered silent in the company of strangers, made no great impression on his family, but she did on George and the feeling was mutual. When she had first visited London with Emily she had been content to amuse herself with museums and art galleries. George too would take her to the Royal Academy and the National Gallery, but he would also show her a side to the capital the tourists didn't see. He would give her a glimpse of the kind of parties she could soon be attending and he talked of the people she might be expected to rub shoulders with. Compared to George and his family, she and her sisters lived like dormice and as Charlotte made her way back to Haworth she didn't know whether to be excited or terrified. What was certain is that the trip that summer had taken its toll.

symptoms. As the New Year dawned, Anne was told she was suffering from advanced consumption. There was no cure, but Charlotte was prepared to grasp at any straw. Throughout those tortuous months she had written frequently to George and when he heard of this fresh tragedy, he immediately offered to send a renowned physician and personal friend to examine Anne. For a brief moment, Charlotte allowed herself to hope that this time death wasn't inevitable. Her father, however, knew that no amount of second opinions could change the facts. Patrick had resigned himself to the loss of yet another child and George's kind offer was politely declined. Anne's last wish was to visit the coast and Charlotte, wanting to ensure her sister's final days were as peaceful as possible, agreed and asked Ellen to join them. The sombre party made their way to Scarborough that June. Only two of them returned.

Having seen her only three surviving siblings die within nine months of each other, it was little wonder that Charlotte asked herself why life is sometimes so "blank, bleak and bitter." She had never known the parsonage to be so quiet and now the clock seemed to tick louder than ever marking out the long lonely hours. The days were painful, but the nights even worse. However, even at her lowest point, Charlotte managed to muster some hope for the future.

"Solitude, Remberance and Longing are to be almost my sole companions all day through," she wrote to Ellen. "That at night I shall go to bed with them, that they will long keep me sleepless – that next morning I shall wake to them again…but crushed I am not yet: nor robbed of elasticity, nor of hope, nor quite of endeavour. Still I have some strength to fight the battle of life."

When Emily had become ill Charlotte had put down her pen, but now writing became her whole reason for existing. Sitting down in the dining room listening to the wind blow from the moors and the rain hammer at the windows, she returned to her second novel. She had begun *Shirley* when both of her sisters were alive and when she went back to it now a little of the darkness lifted. There were still days when she felt she had been placed in solitary confinement, but a rigid structure stopped her thinking too much. She ate breakfast at nine o'clock. Once the housework was complete she would take a walk or busy herself writing letters, often to George whose kindness had proved such a comfort. At six o'clock tea would be served. She said prayers with her father at half past eight and by the time the clock struck nine all activity had ceased. As her father and the servants, Tabby and Martha Brown slept, Charlotte returned silently to her writing. Some days she talked to no one outside the house at all and the silence became a deafening reminder of what she had lost. In Haworth everywhere Charlotte looked she saw death and when the town was hit by an outbreak of cholera she grew to fear every cough and sneeze. It was now the height of summer, but Charlotte was not prepared to take any chances. She bought a new fur boa, wrapped it tightly around her neck and prayed it might protect her frail body from disease. By the end of August, Charlotte was still well and *Shirley* was finished. She didn't know whether it was better or worse than *Jane Eyre*, but it was done.

James Taylor, a partner in the publishing house, who Charlotte had written to on a few occasions in the past, offered to come and collect the manuscript. He was going on holiday to Scotland that year and it would, he said, be no trouble to return via Haworth. James was a diligent man, but he also had an ulterior motive. Unbeknown to Charlotte, he had been admiring her from a distance. Their correspondence might have only amounted to a handful of letters, but James had savoured every word. What had started out as a crush had developed into something altogether deeper and he wasn't about to pass up the opportunity to see where the woman he dreamed about spent her days. Charlotte was in no mood for entertaining and did her best to put him off with as many excuses as she could think of. Her father, she said, was too old to be properly hospitable; there was no one to go walking with him on the moors and she was sure that he would soon be bored. Best of all she reminded him that Haworth was difficult to get to and should he manage to navigate the various railways he would find at the end only a "strange uncivilised place". James was not to be dissuaded and while he agreed not to trouble Charlotte by staying overnight, he was resolved on spending an afternoon in her company. It was the end of the first week of September when he arrived. It had been a long journey, but as soon as he stepped foot through the front door, Charlotte ushered him into the dining room and began counting the minutes to his departure. If James was hoping to impress he failed on every count. Having dared to criticise a section in an earlier rough draft of *Shirley*, he already had a black mark against his name. When he looked at her, she recoiled and while there was little James could do about it, with his red hair and pale skin he also bore an unfortunate resemblance to Branwell, the brother who had caused Charlotte so much pain.

"He is not ugly, but very peculiar," she wrote to Ellen in the matter of fact way that only she could. "The lines in his face show an inflexibility and – I must add a hardness – which do not attract."

James seemed not to notice when Charlotte winced whenever he opened his mouth and concluded as only those blinded by love can that the visit had been a resounding success. As he made his way

Following the discovery of spa water, Scarborough became a popular destination for those hoping to benefit from its healing properties. However the sea air was not enough to cure Charlotte's sister Anne, who died at the resort.

The Gun Group Portrait by an unknown engraver shows the Brontë siblings in happier times. Now Charlotte had only her own thoughts for company.

back to London he had the new manuscript by Currer Bell under his arm and a definite warm glow in his heart.

The follow-up to *Jane Eyre* was eagerly awaited, but despite the growing interest Charlotte still insisted on using her pseudonym. George had reluctantly agreed, but having read *Shirley*, whose characters had been unashamedly taken from real life, he and his colleagues doubted she would remain anonymous for long. As the curates and mill owners of Yorkshire began to read about themselves in print they also began to speculate as to who was the real Currer Bell. With rumours closing in, Charlotte grew paranoid. She was convinced letters and proofs from the publishers were being secretly opened and desperate to escape the gossip of the town and the silence of the house, she made plans to visit London. George had insisted that she should be a guest at his family home and determined this time to fit in, Charlotte sent for a dressmaker. While the idea of London still made her nervous and she worried about who she might meet and what she might say, at least now she wouldn't have to fret about a frayed hemline.

Through the many letters they had written to each other, George and Charlotte's friendship had blossomed and she now felt she could talk to him about anything. She had asked his advice about where best to invest the money she had made from *Jane Eyre*, they had talked about the books they had read and the authors they admired. George genuinely cared for Charlotte and after all she had gone through he was determined that when she came to London she would put her worries, at least for a few weeks, to one side.

He was true to his word. With George by her side, Charlotte visited an exhibition of JMW Turner's watercolours, they went to see the productions of *Macbeth* and *Othello* everyone had raved about, they toured the new Houses of Parliament and one night, George told her he had invited a very special guest to dinner. William Makepeace Thackeray. Charlotte was petrified. She knew George would do his best to make her feel at ease, but she also knew his moral support might not be enough. On paper she could express herself eloquently, rarely stopping to think whether what she said was appropriate or insulting. She just wrote. However, in company her wit deserted her and the loud passionate voice of her novels was silenced. Charlotte knew what the literary world wanted from Currer Bell was flamboyance, someone who could walk into a room and make heads turn, she also knew that with her they would always be disappointed. For George's sake, she did her best not to look terrified. He had invited Thackeray because he knew how much she admired him. Charlotte tried to put on a brave face, but it was no good, as one of those she met would later remark, "the little lady looked tired with her own brains." Charlotte thought too much. When she was alone with George she found she could relax, but every other outing was an exhausting trial. There was also another irritant. James Taylor. Whenever she looked round, he seemed to be there, his unpleasant little face staring at hers. Despite feeling a little tired, Charlotte did manage to summon the strength to write yet another damning character analysis of a man whose features she was sure could quite easily cause milk to curdle.

"He tries to be very kind and even to express sympathy sometimes, but he does not manage it," she told Ellen. "He has a determined dreadful nose in the middle of his face which when poked into my countenance cuts into my soul like iron." Quite where Charlotte would have preferred his nose other than in the middle of his face, she never said, but the more James tried to please her, the more he annoyed her. George, however, had to do very little to make Charlotte smile. She stayed two weeks in London and by the end of the fortnight, her friendship with him had turned into something much more intimate. Back in Haworth she continued as she had always done to sign her letters to him as Currer Bell, but the formality which had marked their early correspondence was gone. She teased him about being a man of business and poked fun at the fashionable company he kept. While Charlotte's anonymity was gradually being eroded in the real world, her alias still offered some protection. Writing to George as Currer Bell she told herself she wasn't an older woman flirting with a younger man, but simply an author amusing her publisher. As the first anniversary of Emily's death approached, her flirtatious letters to George were a welcome distraction.

It was early the following year when Currer Bell was finally unmasked. Charlotte heard many stories of those in Haworth who had never read a book before borrowing a copy of *Shirley* by the celebrity author who lived just a few streets away. She was told Arthur Bell Nicholls had taken to reading the book alone in his room and on numerous occasions had been overheard roaring with laughter.

She had also caught him reading scenes, which poked fun at the double standards and general ignorance of many young curates, aloud to Patrick and when he finished both would nod their heads in knowing agreement. Arthur was sure he had been the inspiration for *Shirley's* Mr McCarthy and he could find no fault with the portrayal. In truth, he was flattered to have made any impression at all on Charlotte. However, if he thought making it into the pages of one of her books meant he had finally been noticed, he was wrong.

It would take Charlotte many years to see him as anything other than a dull but hardworking curate.

With Charlotte's secret out and the reaction almost universally favourable, she was finally set to enter literary society. It was a place which had been hard won and George was more than ready to show off his firm's brightest and best discovery. Charlotte still needed some convincing, but when strangers began to appear in the parsonage grounds hopeful of a glimpse of the woman everyone said was Currer Bell, her father encouraged her to escape for a while to London. While she declined an offer to stay with friends in favour of an invite from George, Charlotte continued to tell herself the feelings she had for him were ones of simple respect and admiration. Her friend Ellen was not so sure. She read the letters which heaped compliment after compliment on the young publisher and began to suspect Charlotte wanted more from George than friendship or a brotherly replacement for Branwell. Charlotte predictably quashed such romantic suggestions, but during her stay in London even George's mother, who now knew her real identity, couldn't help noticing there was more to their relationship than the business of books.

She couldn't understand what George saw in her, they were opposites in every way. He was good looking, affable and had a bright future in business ahead of him. She was almost paranoid about her lack of beauty, her own social awkwardness made others feel uncomfortable and while she clearly had some talent for writing she was still a poor parson's daughter.

Charlotte would probably have agreed, but when she was with George, those differences seemed not to matter. While other less scrupulous publishers would have thought nothing of parading her as an exhibit in a literary freak show, George knew Charlotte still had to be handled with care. He took her to the Ladies Gallery of the House of Commons and together they attended Sunday service at the Chapel Royal where George knew she would be able to catch sight of one of her childhood heroes the Duke of Wellington. Despite still feeling physically inferior to the many ladies she saw gracing the arms of gentlemen, George even managed to persuaded her to sit for a portrait, a gift he said for her father. The trip wasn't free from social disasters. There were still the dinner parties when guests arrived hoping to meet a brilliant conversationalist and left with nothing at all to boast to their friends about and other evenings when Charlotte seemed determined to blend into even the plainest of wallpaper. However, while others felt cheated, George did not. Whenever she talked about leaving, he persuaded her to stay and a fortnight turned into three weeks and then a month. Charlotte knew she would have to go back soon, but before she did, George invited her to Scotland. He and his sister were going to collect their younger brother from school and he asked if Charlotte would like to join them. It would mean cutting short a planned visit to Ellen, but Charlotte didn't need to be asked twice. By the time she wrote to her friend she already had the excuses prepared. George, she said, had been very persuasive and having set his heart on showing her the Highlands and Edinburgh she didn't like to disappoint him. Mrs Smith, who was feeling increasing unease about her son's relationship, had made her disapproval of the journey clear, but Charlotte insisted her concerns were unjustified. She and George were friends, no more, no less and that was the way it would always remain.

"Now I believe that George and I understand each other very

Following the death of her brother and two sisters,
Charlotte returned to her writing, penning Shirley in the
quiet dining room which had once been a hive of activity.

well, and respect each other sincerely," she wrote to Ellen who must have thought she had been here all before. "We both know the wide breach time has made between us; we do not embarrass each other, or very rarely, my six or eight years of seniority to say nothing of the lack of all pretension to beauty etc, are a perfect safeguard."

Just as she had insisted Monsieur Heger was a man she respected as a tutor and nothing else, so now she did her best to deny her real feelings for George. She had to. She cared for him deeply, but she had convinced herself he would never think of her the same way. She may have written about intellect triumphing over beauty in *Jane Eyre*, but in the real world she knew she wasn't pretty or well connected enough to be his wife. If she allowed herself to think for just one moment that she and George could ever be more than just friends, she feared the disappointment when it inevitably came would be too much to bear. Charlotte couldn't risk her world falling apart again, but she was at the top of a slide and stopping herself reaching the bottom would be easier said than done.

Charlotte did cancel part of the trip to Scotland, but she couldn't deny herself completely and agreed instead to meet them later in Edinburgh. They were two of the happiest days she ever had. George hired a driver who knew every part of the city. He took them to the places made famous by Walter Scott, they walked up the Royal Mile to the castle grounds and from the top of Arthur's Seat they looked out across Prince's Street and the New Town.

When she returned to Haworth, many miles away from George, she was visibly downhearted. Patrick was not slow to diagnose the cause of her depression and feared it would now only be a matter of time before he lost his daughter to George and to London. Charlotte's mask of propriety was slipping. Just as she had anxiously waited for letters from Monsieur Heger so now she waited for those written in George's hand. Thankfully he was a little more forthcoming in his correspondence and while there was major building work going on at the parsonage, nothing could disturb Charlotte as she devoured each line. With each new letter, her feelings for him grew and she couldn't resist showing off his talents. Copies of his letters were sent to Ellen and Charlotte talked endlessly of his fine mind and happy temperament. With a distance between them, Charlotte could just about keep up the pretence, but when George invited her on holiday to the Rhine she knew whatever decision she made would colour the future of their entire relationship. Ellen felt forced to point out some pretty obvious home truths.

When Charlotte admitted that if she went, "all London would gabble like a countless host of geese", Ellen told her the gossip would have some foundation. No young good looking bachelor would ask a single woman to go on holiday, unless he hoped to bring back a little souvenir of his own. It wasn't what Charlotte wanted to hear and she still insisted his intentions were entirely platonic.

"I think you draw great conclusions from small inference," she told Ellen. "Were there no vast barrier of age, fortune, etc, there is perhaps enough personal regard to make things possible which are now impossible. If men and women married because they like each others' temper, look, conversation, nature and so on – and if besides, years were more nearly equal – the chance you allude to might be admitted as a chance – but other reasons regulate matrimony – reasons of convenience, of connection, of money. Meantime I am content to have him as a friend – and pray God to continue to me the common-sense to look on one so young, so rising and so hopeful in no other light."

Just the thought of going with George to the Rhine sent Charlotte into a fever. While everyone else, including her father and Ellen, believed he was on the brink of proposing, Charlotte simply couldn't accept he loved her in the same way she loved him. She already knew her heart was not made of granite and if she was to prevent George from breaking it, she had to summon a "quiet wisdom and strength…to resist the lure of pleasure when it comes in such shape as our better judgment disapproves."

Charlotte didn't know what to do. She desperately wanted to go away with George, but knew it might be disastrous. Sinking again into a depression, the pressure of delivering her third book also weighed heavy on her shoulders. Relief now came from the unlikeliest of quarters. James Taylor knew she was struggling and while Charlotte would have never described them as good friends, they had unexpectedly grown a little closer over the past few months. Looking for an excuse to write to her regularly, James had begun sending copies of the weekly literary magazine *Athenaeum* to Haworth. He said he hoped it would provide her with some amusement and Charlotte appreciated his efforts. She realised his correspondence was probably born out of something other than simple diligence, but she was forced to admit that may be her first impressions of him had been a little harsh.

"You may laugh as much and as wickedly as you please," she told Ellen. "But the fact is there is a quiet constancy about this, my diminutive and red-haired friend, which adds a foot to his stature – turns his sandy locks dark, and altogether dignifies him a good deal in my estimation."

For someone she had previously referred to as "the little man" this was praise indeed. Freed from actually having to be in the same room, Charlotte had come to respect James, but still consumed by her feelings for George, thoughts of him occupied little of her time. It would have probably remained that way had she not received a letter telling her he was soon to leave for India. George needed him to go there on business and knowing that he might be away five years or more he was desperate to see her.

Charlotte remembered the first time he had come to the parsonage, how he had hung on her every word and now as she looked back at his many letters she knew there was only one reason for his visit. James was going to ask her to marry him. Arriving flustered a few weeks later, his nervous face confirmed his intention. James didn't go into much detail about his posting to India, except to say it was "necessary to the continued prosperity of the business" and that while he would miss England it was his duty as a partner in the firm. For much of the time he was silent, unable to find the words he so dearly wanted to say. For a moment Charlotte thought he might return to London his heart unburdened. However, as he went to leave, knowing this was his last chance, he finally plucked up the courage to talk of marriage. As he did, Charlotte braced herself.

"As he stood near me, as he looked at me in his keen way, it was all I could do to stand my ground tranquilly and steadily, and not to recoil as before. It is no use saying anything if I am not candid – I avow then, that on this occasion, predisposed as I was to regard him very favourably – his manner and his personal presence scarcely pleased me more than at the first interview."

It wasn't the most memorable of proposals. James looked visibly embarrassed and when he was done he gave Charlotte a book, told her to treasure it and hoped he would hear from her soon. When he left it took a minute or two for what had happened to sink in. Marriage to James was unthinkable. At least that's what she had told herself as she watched him leave. However, in the days after his departure Charlotte began to doubt whether she had made the right decision. Her father certainly seemed keen, praising him as the kind of man who would make a solid and respectable husband. Charlotte didn't doubt that one of the main reasons for her father's sudden enthusiasm was the knowledge that if she did marry it would guarantee him at least another five years with her in Haworth. However, when Smith Williams wrote at length praising James's good character, the idea of becoming his wife didn't seem quite so ludicrous. She wasn't in love with him, but nor did she desire his love. It would in the least romantic sense be a partnership of equals. Charlotte began to wonder whether in five years time she might be grateful to have any husband at all, even if it was James. However, every time she wavered, Charlotte reminded herself what love was and what marriage should be. She had loved Monsieur Heger; she loved George, not with the same intensity perhaps, but it was still love. Whatever feelings she might have in time for James they would never be of the passionate kind.

"An absence of five years," she wrote to Ellen, almost thinking aloud. "A dividing expanse of three oceans — the wide difference between a man's active career and a woman's passive existence — these things are almost equivalent to an eternal separation — But there is another thing which forms a barrier more difficult to pass than any of these. Would Mr T and I ever suit? Could I ever feel for him enough love to accept of him as a husband? Friendship, gratitude, esteem I have, but each moment he came near me — and that I could see his eyes fastened on me – my veins ran ice."

She had answered her own question, but over the days and weeks which followed, Charlotte continued to agonise about the proposal. Finally she concluded she had made the right decision.

"Were I to marry him my heart would bleed in pain and humiliation," she told Ellen. "I could not – could not – look up to him. No, if Mr T be the only husband Fate offers to me, single I must always remain."

Just before James had announced his departure to India, Charlotte had been contemplating a trip to London. She briefly thought about calling off the plans to concentrate on finishing her third novel, *Villette*, but the book was set aside when George wrote to tell her he was now too busy and would have to cancel the trip they had planned for that summer.

Charlotte immediately wrote back mustering as much blasé spirit as she could. She told him that while she was disappointed for his sake, she had already decided not to go to the Rhine. It was, she said, the kind of pleasure she had not yet earned. However, she also told him that she was "sedulously cool and nonchalant" about seeing him again. Nothing could have been further from the truth. When he asked if she could come a day earlier so they could attend a lecture Thackeray was giving, she immediately said yes and nine days after James left for India Charlotte arrived in London.

Her train pulled into the station at ten o'clock at night and she was met on the platform by George and his mother. He looked a lot older than she remembered and worries of work were now etched on his once youthful face. She was reminded of his old self the evening they went to Crystal Palace. The Great Exhibition had opened a few weeks before and was attracting visitors from across the British Empire. Charlotte was not as easily impressed as most by the display of industrial prowess, but with George she laughed at all the unnecessary extravagance. That evening was to be a rare moment of happiness during an otherwise painful visit. George played the dutiful host when he could, but his business was taking up more and more of his time and often Charlotte found herself alone. Without him around London was a lot less fun and it was then that she came to an awful realisation. Whatever hopes she had secretly harboured about George as she watched him now she knew she was no longer a priority in his life. Charlotte was sure he still enjoyed the time they spent together, but something had changed since that casual invitation to the Rhine all those months ago. The warmth he still showed her was genuine, but now she saw it was the same warmth which he extended to a dozen other people. Charlotte wasn't sure whether George had finally fallen under the influence of his mother or whether it was she who had mistaken his relentless flirting for something more meaningful. What she did know was that whatever Ellen and her father thought, George wasn't about to propose.

"You seem to think me in such a happy, enviable position," she wrote to Ellen while still in London. "Pleasant moments I have, but it is usually a pleasure I am obliged to repel and check, which cannot benefit the future, but only add to its solitude, which is no more to be relied on than the sunshine of one summer's day. I pass portions of many a night in extreme sadness."

Charlotte had learnt the hard way that with unrequited love the only outcome is heartbreak. Convinced now that George did not love her, she knew she had to push him away. The pain she felt in doing so was great, but it was nothing to the pain she would feel if she allowed herself for just one moment to hope his mind and his heart could be changed. She couldn't risk her own heart being broken again and the more she thought about it the more Charlotte convinced herself she was right. If she had learnt anything over the last few years it was that there was nothing more admirable than a single woman. She knew she couldn't rely on George to make her happy and with James now making his way to India her only option was to find solace within herself.

Those Charlotte couldn't have she had longed for, those who offered themselves to her she had turned away. In *Jane Eyre*, Charlotte had written of love conquering all, but in her experience happy endings seemed only to exist in the pages of books. She was resigned to growing old single and lonely.

4.   The Triumph of Love

"Love comforteth like sunshine after rain."
William Shakespeare

Everything and yet nothing had changed. It had been five years since Charlotte's name had first made it into print, five years in which she had realised and surpassed all her literary ambitions. However, as her manuscript of *Villette* was being scrutinised in London, there was little of the eager expectation which she had felt on the publication of *Jane Eyre*.

Despite the success and critical acclaim, Charlotte still felt marooned on the same endless cycle of dashed promises and disappointment. Fame had only increased her insecurities. It had shown her new doors of opportunity, but when opened all she had found were more places where she didn't fit in.

Growing up neither rich or poor, Charlotte had no affinity with either the cottage dwellers of Haworth who struggled to make ends meet or the middleclass manufacturing families, whose grand houses and factories stood as bold testaments to their new found wealth. Later as books and writing had become as necessary to her as food and water she should have excelled as a governess. However, she had been unable to convey her passion, despising many of her pupils and hating the monotony she believed turned learning into a daily grind. Charlotte had always told herself that if she could become a writer, her problems would be solved. She would finally have friends equal to her in intelligence and who understood the importance and power of the written word. *Jane Eyre* had been a passport to that high society, but she had felt equally uncomfortable in the grand dining rooms of London as she had in the classrooms of Roe Head. As she looked back on her life she realised she had always yearned for something other than what she had. George had done his best to smooth her path to literary greatness, but kind words had failed to turn Charlotte into the pretty social butterfly she sometimes so desperately wanted to be.

A law unto herself, George had now grown used to the deadlines which came and went without so much as one new chapter being finished and the letters which explained how some fresh torment had prevented her from putting pen to paper. Charlotte remained the jewel in Smith, Elder & Co's publishing crown, but their star author's erratic workflow and demand for feedback which was then promptly ignored now meant George had good cause on more than one occasion to quietly curse the name of Currer Bell.

However, *Villette* had finally been finished and Charlotte had promised to visit London before Christmas to make the final corrections. This time the trip would definitely be more about business than pleasure. Charlotte felt sure most of her days would be taken up with work, but she told herself she was happy for the book to be her priority and George when she did see him to just be a friend.

Until then there was much to occupy her in Haworth. December was always a busy month for her father. Christmas had a habit of boosting the numbers attending Sunday service. Unfamiliar faces, who hadn't set foot in church since Easter, squeezed into the pews and said their prayers so quietly no-one would notice when they got the words wrong. The parsonage itself was no less busy with a steady stream of visitors, keen to pass on their festive best wishes. Charlotte didn't mind. With her manuscript completed she was more than happy to help Tabby and Martha with the housework and after so many months of silence it was good to hear the house alive with the sound of voices. By the time night fell and the well-wishers had gone, life reverted to its usual quiet routine.

Charlotte would sit down to eat dinner with her father and more often than not they would be joined by Arthur. Afterwards Patrick and his curate would catch up with the day's events, they would talk at length about progress at the National School which had become Arthur's pride and joy and with a busy schedule of services ahead, there was much to discuss.

Charlotte, who had always found the minutiae of clerical life impossibly dull, was more than happy to leave them to it.

The Monday evening of December 13, 1852 began the same as any other. The dinner plates were cleared, Charlotte politely made her excuses, Patrick lit his pipe and for the first time that day he began to relax. Arthur, however, who had much more pressing things on his mind than school admissions or church rates struggled to unwind. For months he had watched Charlotte from afar. He had seen her struggle to come to terms with the death of her beloved sister Emily and had admired her as she quietly went back to her writing with a single-minded determination not to be beaten. There were times when he had been about to reach out and put a

Arthur Bell Nicholls had been a presence at the parsonage for years. What Charlotte didn't know was that he had fallen in love with her and his passion would turn her life upside down. (courtesy of the Brontë Society)

comforting hand on her shoulder, but at the last minute had stopped himself. Summoning more will power than he ever thought he possessed Arthur had tried to carry on as normal. He hadn't quite succeeded. Charlotte had not been entirely oblivious to his brooding presence and neither had her father. However, with both convinced Arthur would never give voice to whatever feelings he had they turned a blind eye to the "constant looks", his "strange feverish restraint" and hoped it was simply an unfortunate phase.

Patrick had always liked Arthur. He had found him to be an able and dedicated curate, but the idea of him becoming a permanent member of his family was unthinkable. Charlotte was now his only child, she was also a famous author who he felt deserved much better than marriage to a poor clergyman.

Had Arthur ever once doubted his feelings for Charlotte, he might have been persuaded to keep quiet. However, he knew what he felt was real. He had struck a bargain with himself not to say anything until she had finished *Villette*. With the book done he steeled himself. His love for Charlotte might have grown without even the slightest encouragement, but now his heart felt like it was about to burst. He was going to propose and however painful the consequences might be he would withstand them.

Leaving Patrick alone in his study, Arthur stood for a moment in the dimly lit hallway. Charlotte, who had been busying herself in the dining room, heard him get ready to leave. She didn't look at the clock, but reckoning it must be some time between eight and nine she put down her book and listened out for the sound of the front door shutting behind him. Nothing. She listened again, but instead of the latch closing, there was a knock on the dining room door. It was only the gentlest of taps, but to Charlotte it was like lightning.

In that moment she knew there was no way of stopping what was about to happen next. Opening the door, she saw Arthur stood in the shadows. Moving into the light, Charlotte couldn't help noticing that he looked very different to the confident man she had often seen leading his congregation in prayer. Against his thick black hair and the dark eyebrows which always made him look so serious, his skin looked deathly pale. Trembling, his low voice cracked as he struggled to get the words out. Arthur was more nervous than Charlotte had seen any man before. He had spent weeks pacing his bedroom trying to decide exactly what it was he should say, but no amount of practice could have prepared him for that night. Standing in front of the woman he had fallen hopelessly in love with, Arthur knew he was about to put his heart and quite possibly his career on the line.

He told her of the months he had spent nurturing even the smallest hope that she might love him too. Shaking from head to foot he begged her to think seriously about being his wife and assured her that should she find it in her heart to agree, he would not disappoint her.

When he had finished, he looked to Charlotte hoping for some words of comfort or at the very least a look of gentle understanding. She was speechless. Charlotte didn't hear every word Arthur uttered that night, but when he had finished she was in no doubt that he was the man who loved her deeply. This wasn't a throwaway proposal from a Henry Nussey or a David Bryce. Nor was it the kind of well-meant but jaw-droppingly practical proposal of a James Taylor. No, this was something else altogether.

It took Arthur just a few minutes to confess his love, but his proposal was more passionate and more keenly felt than Charlotte had ever expected.

"He made me for the first time feel what it costs a man to declare affection where he doubts the response," she wrote to Ellen the following day, still in shock at the events of the previous evening. "The spectacle of one ordinarily so statue-like, thus trembling, stirred and overcome, gave me a kind of strange shock. He spoke of sufferings he had borne for months, of sufferings he could endure no longer and craved leave for some hope…"

Charlotte knew exactly how Arthur felt. She had begged Monsieur Heger to throw her some crumb of hope and when he refused, her entire world had been sent into turmoil. Now in Arthur she saw those very same emotions replayed. He had not only fallen in love with her, but he was prepared to sacrifice everything to be with her. There was just one problem. Charlotte didn't love him. She never had. It had been seven and a half years since Arthur had first arrived in Haworth and during all that time, she had never felt one spark of attraction. She liked Arthur, yes. He was kind and more thoughtful than most people she had ever known. Often when she saw him she remembered how he had conducted Emily's funeral with such quiet grace and how afterwards he had lifted her sister's dog Flossie into his arms to stop her running after the cortege.

She knew also that Arthur cared deeply for her father and he had already gone out of his way to encourage him to take things a little easier. There was she realised very little to dislike about him, but could she really spend the rest of her life with a man who had never once made her heart skip a beat?

In the past Charlotte would have instantly dismissed the idea. She would have told him immediately that they were unsuited and sent him on his way. Not now. The last few years had taught her the real meaning of loneliness and the often fleeting nature of happiness.

Charlotte needed time to gather her thoughts. Whatever her opinion of Arthur, his proposal deserved more than a hurried 'no'. She needed to be alone. Realising her father could walk into the room at any minute, Charlotte panicked. She took hold of Arthur, ushered him along the hallway and after promising to give him an answer the next day, she put him out like a cat into the cold winter night.

Having closed the front door, Charlotte stood for a moment wondering what to do next. Taking a deep breath, she walked into her father's study and told him without going into any more detail than absolutely necessary that his curate also wanted to be her husband. Charlotte didn't get the chance to explain that she wasn't in love with Arthur and even if she had it would have done no good. Patrick was in no mood to listen. Seeing the proposal as a betrayal and Arthur's failure to ask for his daughter's hand further proof of his unsuitability, his anger boiled over and in his rage the very foundations of the house seemed to shake. Patrick was now in his seventies, his health was not good and having buried his wife and five of his children, he was determined not to lose his only surviving daughter to another man. The thought of being left alone was too much for Patrick to bear. Unable to admit his own selfish, but entirely understandable, reasons for wanting to prevent the marriage, he instead railed against the idea of a poor curate thinking he was a worthy suitor for one of English literature's most famous names. For all Arthur's good qualities, Patrick believed he simply didn't deserve a woman like Charlotte. She was successful, despite all the odds she had made her name in a notoriously fickle world and the future might well bring even greater rewards. What had Arthur done? In Haworth he may have won the respect of the parishioners he quietly served, but in Patrick's eyes, a few decent

The winter was often harsh in Haworth, but when Arthur Nicholls proposed to Charlotte the atmosphere inside the parsonage was equally frosty.

sermons and improving educational standards weren't enough to make him a suitable husband for his daughter. That night the usual quiet calm of the parsonage was shattered. Charlotte watched as the veins on her father's temples bulged with anger and his eyes became bloodshot with fury. He could barely comprehend Arthur's insolence. To Patrick the proposal was both a personal slight and sign of a rash and stupid man who had clearly lost his mind.

Charlotte may well have agreed with much of what her father said, but she couldn't bear the venom with which it was delivered. His character assassination of Arthur she saw as both unfair and unjust. As she listened to him rail, every sentence seemed to compound the hurt. Unable to reason with him, Charlotte eventually left her father's study and went upstairs. She knew there was little chance of sleeping, but as she lay on the bed her eyes wide open she tried to make some sense of what had happened.

Her father had been unnecessarily unkind, cruel even. However, she also knew that had she loved Arthur, those insults would have been like daggers to her heart, but she didn't and they weren't. Charlotte had waited all her life for someone to tell her they loved her above everything else. She knew Arthur had meant every word he had spoken, but she didn't feel the same and knew she probably never would. There was only one thing she could do. The next morning she would thank Arthur for his proposal, but she would also tell him that for both their future sanity she could not marry him.

It was thirteen years since Charlotte had received the letter from Henry Nussey asking her to be his wife. That rejection had been delivered without a second thought; turning down Arthur would not be so easy. Charlotte knew how it felt to be on the wrong side of unrequited love and she was determined to treat his raw emotions with more sympathy and care than Monsieur Heger had treated her own. She may not have been able to return his feelings, but she did feel enormous pity for a man who had the strength of character to open his heart knowing it might very well be broken.

Whatever her father said, Arthur was neither a bad man nor a fool. Charlotte had never had much time for curates, but since she had so successfully ridiculed the profession in *Shirley*, her mood had softened. Now she remembered the time when Patrick had fallen ill and how Arthur had stepped in without complaint. Without anyone asking him to, he had taken on more responsibility, worked longer hours and all the while he had never been short of a kind word. He had shown himself to be a decent, hard-working man, who had cared for Patrick like he was his own father, but now all that seemed to count for nothing. Charlotte had learnt a long time ago that sometimes the decent people in life don't always get the good fortune they deserve and she knew she was about to consign Arthur to that unfortunate number.

The next morning Charlotte wrote to Arthur to tell him she could not marry him and Patrick, whose temper had not been calmed by the dawn of a new day, demanded his immediate resignation. Arthur was not completely surprised by Patrick's reaction, but having lost the woman he loved, finding new employment was the least of his worries. Heartbroken, he avoided the church at all cost and spent most of his days and all of his evenings in his room. Hardly eating, he lay on his bed and wondered how it had all come to this; how his quiet, ordinary existence had been so brutally torn apart. He couldn't face seeing anyone, which was probably just as well as his proposal had quickly become the talk of

Haworth. Some, siding with Patrick, muttered disapproval, others asked after the likeable curate and hoped the matter would soon be forgotten. All wondered what would happen next.

Arthur himself wasn't quite sure, but he knew that without Charlotte, staying in Haworth was impossible. He wrote to Patrick and formally handed in his resignation. What he didn't know as he penned that letter was that a few hundred yards away, Charlotte's sense of injustice was growing. Watching her father mobilise opposition against Arthur, she tried to shut her ears to the continued spite which seemed to sit so uneasily on the lips of a devoutly religious man. Whenever it seemed Patrick had run out of insults he found some new source of abuse, but the more he railed against Arthur, the more Charlotte felt compelled to leap to his defence.

She was thirty-six-years-old, but her father's damning appraisal of Arthur turned her into a rebellious teenager resolved to think exactly the opposite. Without knowing it, over the coming weeks and months, Patrick would fuel his daughter's feelings for a man she had herself said she had no intention of marrying.

"They don't understand the nature of his feelings," Charlotte told Ellen. She was now writing to her every day, keeping her informed of a situation which seemed to change hour by hour. "But I see now what they are. Mr N is one of those who attach themselves to very few whose sensations are close and deep – like an underground street, running strong but in a narrow channel. He continues restless and ill – he carefully performs the occasional duty – but does not come near the church, procuring a substitute every Sunday."

As the New Year came the scandal showed no sign of blowing over. Rumours of Arthur's fragile mental state had grown over that Christmas. His appetite had still not recovered and all offers of a

Patrick Brontë was now an old man. He had buried five of his six children and worried about his own future; he made his feelings about Charlotte finding a husband very clear.

shoulder to cry on had been refused. Unwilling to let the matter lie, Charlotte's father had also become impossible to live with. She needed to escape to somewhere no-one knew the name of Arthur Bell Nicholls or the story of his aching heart. London now seemed more desirable than ever.

In all that had happened since Arthur's proposal, Charlotte had barely thought about George or her new novel which was awaiting a final read through. Now it provided a perfect excuse to get away and towards the end of the first week in January, Charlotte packed her bags and headed south. As the factories and industrial landscape of her home disappeared into the distance, she allowed herself to breathe a small sigh of relief. For weeks all she had heard was the sound of her father's continued raging and while most people had been too polite to even mention his name in her company, she knew Arthur was all anyone wanted to talk about. Finally she was alone with only her own thoughts for company and it felt good. With *Villette* due to be published in a few weeks she was grateful for the chance to immerse herself in a fictional world again. Amending proofs was a laborious task, but after recent events Charlotte now relished the mundane and the boring. She knew George was not entirely happy with the finished book, but he had stopped short of ordering major changes. It had been him who had suggested using the characters of Cornhill as inspiration, but he had failed to hide his disappointment when presented with the final manuscript. He had at first delighted in his portrayal as the affable and charming Dr John and as he read the early chapters he had understandably become convinced he was to have a starring role. However, when the final volume arrived and he saw his character condemned as superficial, worthy only as a husband to the pretty, but unremarkable Paulina,

George had been less pleased. He had accused Charlotte of horribly misjudging Dr John. He had told her he could never have fallen in love with a woman just because she was pretty and he had insisted the reader would find much cause for complaint in the sudden turn of plot. George was genuinely hurt that she had come to see him as a man whose head was so easily turned, but Charlotte refused to listen to his criticism. In *Villette* she had written off any possibility of a relationship with George and her unwillingness to provide the kind of happy ending which had so delighted the readers of *Jane Eyre* was a sign her idealised romantic notions were no more. Charlotte knew that by using their friendship as source material she risked alienation, but in Haworth she had no regrets about the character of Dr John and she had left Mrs Smith to draw her own conclusions about the novel's portrayal of an overbearing mother content to live out her own ambitions through her son.

Arriving in London, Charlotte became slightly more uneasy about the impact the book might have had on the family, but she soon realised whatever complaints George had were in the past and more pressing problems were now occupying his time. Charlotte had known his firm was struggling financially, he had said as much in his letters. However, caught up first with finishing *Villette* and then with the problem of what to do with Arthur and her warring father, she hadn't realised quite how much strain he had been under. It had only been six months or so since she had last seen him, but he was almost unrecognisable. The young good-looking George she had first met nearly fours years before was no more. The pressure of work had etched itself onto his once handsome face.

"Hard work is telling early," she told Ellen. "Both his complexion, his countenance and the very lines of his features are altered – it is rather the remembrance of what he was than the fact of what he is which can warrant the picture I have been accustomed to give of him. One feels pained to see a physical alteration of this kind – yet I feel glad and thankful that it is merely physical; as far as I can judge mind and manners have undergone no deterioration – rather, I think the contrary."

Charlotte stayed for a month in London, but she saw George only fleetingly. At first she was just grateful to be away from Haworth and as she began the job of proofreading *Villette* she found she had little spare time; sometimes hours went by without one thought of Arthur creeping to the forefront of her mind. However, when the final amendments had been made, Charlotte knew that she must find someway to keep herself occupied.

Free to do what she pleased she avoided the usual attractions and instead seemed intent on searching out London's underclass. While most other tourists were admiring the collections at the British Museum or watching the changing of the guard at Buckingham Palace, she embarked on her own decidedly macabre tour of the capital.

Seeming to take delight in doing the very opposite of what her hosts expected, Charlotte went to Pentonville Prison. Much had been written about the model gaol which had opened a little over ten years before. She had read about its insistence on solitary confinement and how in the exercise yard the inmates were forced to wear cloth bags over the heads to prevent even the slightest communication. Even the high grey walls were intimidating and Charlotte suspected nothing good could ever lay behind them.

Another day she sought out an orphanage knowing those who found themselves in its care rarely prospered and to complete the depressing picture she finished off her tour with a trip to Bethlehem Hospital. Known to most as Bedlam, the asylum which dated back to the reign of Henry VII had been notorious for its brutal treatment of patients. The practice of allowing visitors to wander the cells poking the poor unfortunates with sticks had only recently been stopped, but there was still an element of the freak show to the wards and it wasn't a place for a single woman to linger long.

Seeing those whose lives were a great deal harder than her own put her worries in perspective and despite her peculiar choice of tourist attractions, in her many letters to Ellen, Charlotte seemed relatively content.

However, the joy she had once found in London and George had gone. Having suppressed any feelings she had for him, she now saw him simply as a man with a business to save and his own family to support. He could still be utterly charming, but during the odd evening they spent together there was only a fragile remnant of the closeness they had once enjoyed. As she travelled back home, Charlotte realised there was nothing left for her in London. As the train pulled into the station at Leeds she knew in a few hours she would be home and that she could run away no more.

As she travelled those final few miles she wondered what had happened to Arthur since she had left. She knew her father hadn't yet succeeded in hounding him out of the town, but any hope she had that time might have soothed his temper was soon disappointed.

With many lonely hours to think about Arthur's proposal that previous December, Patrick had become even more hardened against his curate. He had asked himself time and again what could have made an apparently sensible man behave so rashly and the conclusions he had drawn were not flattering.

Arthur, he told Charlotte, wasn't some dashing army officer or wealthy irresponsible chancer who might be expected to go around handing out proposals of marriage with little thought of the consequences.

Arthur was a curate, a man whose entire profession was built on not simply preaching Christian values, but living by them. Patrick knew Arthur may not have been able to help falling in love with Charlotte, but what he couldn't forgive was his pursuit of a wreckless dream. With the campaign against him intensified and with no suggestion that Charlotte would change her mind, Arthur sent for an application form to join the Society for the Propagation of the Gospel. The organisation was responsible for sending missionaries to the four corners of the world. Arthur knew he couldn't stay in Haworth and wanting to be as far away from the town as possible, Australia seemed like as good a place as any.

As he contemplated the next chapter in his own life, Charlotte found some distraction in the reviews for *Villette*. She had worried the novel didn't fit the current fashion for socially aware literature. It contained no great moral about the justice system or criticism of government policy. It was simply a love story. However, the critics, perhaps grateful for a respite from some of the many dreary tomes which then passed for fiction, found much to praise. Some, like George, did find fault with the final volume, but had they only known that Charlotte herself was at that moment involved in a tortuous romance of her own they would have realised that sometimes truth is a great deal stranger than any fiction.

Weeks had gone by since Arthur had first announced his intention to leave, but he still hadn't gone. Some said his missionary papers were still being processed; others suggested he had found another position elsewhere in England. All Charlotte knew was that until he moved out, life could never return to normal.

She didn't doubt his pain, but his refusal to leave was only making things worse and every time she saw the hangdog expression which had become a permanent fixture on his face she couldn't help but feel irritated. Charlotte was still annoyed with her father, but when Arthur insisted on following her up the lane after evening service, looking wistfully as she made her way home, she knew he wasn't helping himself.

Since the proposal, Charlotte and her father had not had much occasion to be in the same room as Arthur. In fact all three had gone out of their way to avoid such a situation. Unfortunately, when the Bishop of Ripon announced he would be visiting Haworth that March they all knew he would expect to see Patrick, his daughter and his curate together. Charlotte would have given anything to hide away in her room, but knowing her absence would have been a slight to their dignified guest she took her place downstairs. It was an uncomfortable situation for all involved and the table of assorted cakes and tarts did nothing to sweeten the atmosphere. Arthur made little effort to hide his hurt. He was tetchy with everyone, particularly Patrick, and as the evening drew to a close he once again tried to prevail on Charlotte to change her mind. She could not bear being in his company a minute longer. She ran upstairs and as she closed her bedroom door she told herself the sooner he was gone the better.

"The fact is I shall be most thankful when he is well away – I pity him, but I do not like that dark gloom of his…If Mr N be a good man at bottom – it is a sad thing that Nature has not given him the faculty to put goodness into a more attractive form."

Charlotte had sat in Haworth Church more times than she could remember, but she had never seen anything so dramatic as the moment Arthur broke down at the pulpit.

Arthur's sullen looks made him appear like a man who had given up on life. Awkward and pale, he talked to few people in the town and even those who had stood by him now found it difficult to muster much sympathy for him. Charlotte saw his fellow curates, not wanting to be tainted by any brush of scandal, shun him and watched in silent pity as his once busy days turned into quiet desolation.

"He & Papa never speak. He seems to pass a desolate life. He has allowed late circumstances so to act on him as to freeze up his manner and overcast his countenance not only to those immediately concerned but every one. He sits drearily in his rooms —If Mr Cartman or Mr Grant or any other clergyman calls to see and as they think to cheer him — he scarcely speaks — I find he tells them nothing — seeks no confidant — rebuffs all attempts to penetrate his mind…He looks ill and miserable. I think and trust in Heaven that he will be better as soon as he fairly gets away from Haworth. He is now grown so gloomy and reserved that nobody seems to like him… Papa has a perfect antipathy to him – and he – I fear – to Papa. Martha hates him – I think he might almost be dying and they would not speak a friendly word to or of him.

"How much of all this he deserves I can't tell, certainly he never was agreeable or amiable, and is less so now than ever…In this state of things I must be and I am entirely passive. I may be losing the purest gem – and to me far the most precious life can give – genuine attachment – or I may be escaping the yoke of a morose temper. In this doubt conscience will not suffer me to take one step in opposition to Papa's will – blended as that will is with the most bitter and unreasonable prejudices."

Arthur still had two months of his notice to serve at Haworth and for Charlotte the days and weeks ticked by slowly. A brief visit to see friends in Manchester and a few days spent with Ellen did little to hurry proceedings along. Finally May arrived. Arthur was leaving and Charlotte couldn't help feeling relieved. Soon she would be able to draw a line under the whole sorry business. They had barely spoken two words to each other since the bishop's visit and convinced Arthur now understood there was no chance of her ever changing her mind she took her seat for the Whitsunday service where he was due to deliver the sermon. Standing at the pulpit, Arthur looked out over the congregation packed into the pews. Normally he paid little notice to who was sat where, but suddenly his gaze became fixated on Charlotte. Knowing in a few days he would no longer be able to look out and see the woman who had captured his heart deep in prayer, he was unable to break his stare.

While Arthur had only previously let his guard down in front of Charlotte now his feelings were on display for everyone to see. Overcome with grief, Arthur faltered over his words. He desperately tried to get to the end of the sermon, but it was no good. His mouth opened, but no words came out and all eyes flicked alternately between Arthur and Charlotte.

It was a scene like none had ever witnessed before. Men of the cloth rarely showed their feelings. Their absolute faith in a higher power seemed to cushion them from the normal heartaches of every day life, but there in front of his parishioners Arthur broke down.

Seeing his obvious pain, some of the women dabbed their eyes while the men looked awkwardly at their shoes. It was painful to watch, but among those who attended church it was only those with the hardest of hearts who failed to feel sorry for a man whose only mistake had been to fall in love.

"He struggled, faltered, then lost command over himself, stood before my eyes and in the sight of all the communicants white, shaking, voiceless," she told Ellen. "Papa was not there thank God!…He made a great effort, but could only with difficulty whisper and falter through the service.

I suppose he thought this would be the last time; he either goes this week or the next. I heard the women sobbing round – and I could not quite check my own tears…I never saw a battle more sternly fought with the feelings than Mr Nicholls fights with his, and when he yields momentarily, you are almost sickened by the sense of the strain upon him. However he is to go, and I cannot speak to him or look at him or comfort him a whit."

Charlotte knew then that she had been wrong about Arthur. As she had watched him grow morose, she had compared her own stoical response to Monsieur Heger's silent rebuffal to Arthur's reaction to rejection and found it wanting.

However, that Whitsunday she realised just how unfair she had been. In the moment he used the pulpit as a crutch, Charlotte understood just how much Arthur must have struggled those past months to keep his emotions in check. She might not have been ready to fall into his arms just yet, but unwittingly Arthur had shown her a side to his character she didn't think existed. Admitting his love for her in the four walls of the parsonage was one thing, but she could think of no other man who would have been moved to expose his feelings so publicly.

A few days later Arthur stood again at the pulpit, this time to take his last service. There was little of the drama of Whitsunday and the mood was subdued. His fellow clergymen from neighbouring parishes had gathered for the low-key send-off. Arthur had taken his duties as a curate seriously. He had worked hard to improve school standards and his tireless efforts had not gone unnoticed. A leaving collection had raised enough money to buy a gold watch and the simple presentation was tinged by sadness. Patrick unsurprisingly was not among those who came to wish him well. However, Arthur bore him no resentment. He knew Patrick too well. He had watched as he had buried his children and struggled with his own health, he may have even understood that however misguided, Patrick just wanted to protect his daughter in the best way he could. Arthur may not have agreed with Patrick's methods, but he understood the motives. When the pair, once so close, but now so distant, sat down to tie up the last loose ends there were no raised voices. The spite and venom of the previous few months had disappeared. Arthur was going and there was nothing more to be said.

Charlotte had decided it was best to keep out of view. She didn't want to make the situation any more painful for Arthur than it already was. With the last of the paperwork complete, she heard him say a final goodbye and listened as he walked out of the parsonage for what would in all likelihood be the very last time. Hidden from view, Charlotte peered out of the window to see him disappear into the night. She saw him walk down the path and she watched as he lingered at the parsonage gate, unable or unwilling to make the final step. Charlotte's resolve crumbled. She might not have loved Arthur, but she couldn't see anyone suffer so much without offering them comfort. She rushed past her father's study and out of the front door.

"He went out thinking he was not to see me," she confided in Ellen. "And indeed till the very last moment I thought it best not. But perceiving that he stayed long before going out the gate, and remembering his long grief, I took courage and went out trembling and miserable. I found him leaning against the garden door in a paroxysm of anguish, sobbing as women never sob. Of course I went straight to him. Very few words were interchanged, those few barely articulate. Several things I should have liked to ask him were swept entirely from my memory. Poor fellow! But he wanted such hope and such encouragement as I could not give him. Still I trust he must know now that I am not cruelly blind and indifferent to his constancy and grief."

The silence was deafening. Charlotte couldn't tell Arthur the one thing he wanted to hear, the one thing which would have help dry his eyes. A few minutes later he was gone.

Early the next morning, Arthur left Haworth. He didn't quite know whether he would ever return or if he would ever see Charlotte again. Back in the parsonage, Arthur's name was never spoken. However, while neither Charlotte nor her father mentioned the man who had turned their lives upside down, both thought about him a lot.

Patrick had grown to depend on Arthur. Until the last few months he had enjoyed his company and looked forward to their evening chats by the fireside. Now he began to realise just how much of the burden of his daily duties Arthur had lifted from his shoulders. A replacement, a man called George de Renzy, had already been appointed, but Patrick knew it would take time for him to learn the correct way, or at least his way, of doing things.

With her father preoccupied, Charlotte busied herself with correspondence. There were dozens of letters from readers and critics which needed to be replied to and George had sent a brand new box of books. However, as much as she tried to fill the hours of the day, she couldn't help wondering if this time she had made a terrible mistake.

All her life had been spent yearning for affection. She had demanded a pure kind of unconditional love, one that words would never be able to fully explain. After Monsieur Heger she had convinced herself that such love didn't exist, but Arthur now made her doubt everything. Charlotte knew he hadn't proposed simply because of her fame or because of any misplaced notion that he really ought to find a wife. Arthur loved her wholly and completely and faced with the one thing she had spent her adult life searching for she had turned her back on it. He may have been a little sullen, serious even, but he loved her, she could see that and all she had given him in return was silent cold rejection. The stress took its toll. A minor cold developed into full blown flu and Charlotte was forced to take to her bed.

However, the worries about her own health were soon overshadowed. Patrick suffered a second stroke. For a time he was completely blind and was forced to rely more than ever on his daughter and the new curate. The prognosis was not good, but Patrick had always been resilient and in time he began to recover, surpassing most medical expectations. As he did both father and daughter realised they missed Arthur more than they ever thought possible. Charlotte knew that while her father had regained some of his independence it would only be a matter of time before she was needed to look after him full-time. It brought into sharp focus how lonely her life could soon be. The last few years had been emotionally draining and Charlotte began to realise that while she had so often railed against the parsonage, describing it as a prison and seeking any opportunity to escape, it was now one of the few familiar and constant things left in her life. While she may not have been able to admit it to anyone else, it was also the only place she truly felt comfortable. With the house eerily quite, the silence punctuated only by the occasional request from her father, Charlotte wondered where all the promise and excitement of the last few years had gone. What she didn't know was that far from packing his bags and moving on to pastures new, Arthur was still waiting in the wings.

It was July when the first letter arrived. His application to become a missionary had he decided been made in haste and faced with the prospect of moving thousands of miles away with no easy way to return, he had withdrawn his application.

Explaining to Charlotte that he had abandoned plans to go to Australia, he also revealed that he was still in Yorkshire. Staying with a friend in nearby Oxenhope, he was waiting to take up a position at Kirk Smeaton some 50 miles from Haworth and given they would be almost neighbours, he wondered if Charlotte might like to write to him. She couldn't help but admire his persistence, but Charlotte remained resolute. Yes she had missed Arthur, yes, he had left a gap that his replacement could never hope to fill, but she still didn't love him. Knowing that he wouldn't require much encouragement to bring up the whole thorny issue of marriage again and just as she had at their last meeting, Charlotte responded with silence. Arthur was undaunted. A second letter arrived, then a third, a fourth and a fifth. Each time Charlotte's response was the same. She couldn't have helped but notice the irony. A few years earlier it had been she who had waited so anxiously for a letter, she who had begged Monsieur Heger to give her some nugget of hope. Now it was Arthur who was watching the post and she the one responsible for his daily disappointment. However, when the sixth letter, written in a similar vein to the previous five, arrived, even Charlotte's iron will could not withstand the onslaught. Her reply was brief, but within those few short lines she gave the green light to Arthur's continued correspondence. The letter may have been completely devoid of the flirtatious style with which she had once written to George, but after months of sleepless nights and mournful days, Arthur was not about to complain about a lack of linguistic flourish.

He saw the door to Charlotte's heart was finally ajar and with both hands he was determined to prise it wide open. Writing in secret and careful to ensure Patrick had no inkling of the letters, Charlotte and Arthur began to write regularly to each other. They weren't great love letters, at least not at the start, but as she told him about events in Haworth and how she and her father were coping, Charlotte began to think what it was she really wanted in life. She had told herself on countless occasions the only reason she had kept coming back to Haworth was because of her father. Certainly he had become more dependent on her and with Martha and Tabby both old themselves, leaving him now would be difficult. However, the truth was Charlotte could have no more left the parsonage for good with his blessing than she could without it.

Confirmation came in a letter from George. It was November, his last letter had arrived around the same time Arthur had got back in contact, but now there seemed to be something he needed to tell her. She read and reread the brief note. Amid the vague terms, inferences and hints, Charlotte was pretty sure George was engaged. She needed to be certain and feeling unable to write to him direct, she sent a letter to his mother. The reply contained all she needed to know. The details hadn't been settled, but George was to be married. He had met Elizabeth Blakeway at a ball that spring and while they had only known her a matter of months they were madly in love and everyone had said what a perfect match they made. Elizabeth was beautiful and as the daughter of a successful London wine merchant a woman of some means. She was as Charlotte had predicted in *Villette*, exactly the kind of woman George would marry and when she finally replied she did so in typical style.

"In great happiness, as in great grief – words of sympathy should be few," she wrote. "Accept my meed of congratulation – and believe me."

Charlotte had told herself time and again that she and George were not meant to be. She had even married him off to someone younger and prettier in *Villette*, but it didn't make the reality any easier to deal with. Now more than ever she needed to talk to Ellen, but her friend had stopped listening. Having discovered a few months earlier that Charlotte was writing to Arthur, the friends who had met all those years ago as teenagers at Margaret Wooler's school had fallen out. Ellen had always been the first to jump to Charlotte's defence, but this time she disapproved and wouldn't be won round. Her reaction was understandable. Charlotte had spent six months pointing out Arthur's defects, telling her she didn't love him and becoming exasperated at his apparent inability to take no for an answer. Now here she was writing to him behind her father's back. Ellen didn't want Charlotte to marry Arthur. In fact she didn't want her to marry anyone. She knew she was likely to remain a spinster and she didn't need Charlotte, her best friend, spoiling her plans by suddenly finding a husband. Without Ellen to advise her, Charlotte decided that she could either stay at Haworth and be lonely or she could stay at Haworth as a married woman. She chose the latter. Now all she had to do was convince her father.

Gathering the courage took weeks, but one evening Charlotte

finally steeled herself. She spoke quietly at first, but as she pointed out how few men would have waited so long for a woman with little wealth and less in the way of looks, she grew in confidence. Patrick didn't want to hear anymore. The thought of another man in the house, the first since the death of his beloved Branwell, remained unthinkable. Charlotte, however, was not to be dissuaded and her father lost the strength or the will to fight her. After a few days, the icy atmosphere in the house thawed. Patrick gave his daughter permission to continue writing to Arthur and the couple's courtship proper began. Charlotte needed to get to know Arthur not as a curate or family friend, but as a future husband and letters alone would not suffice. It was approaching Christmas and in the New Year, Arthur made plans to stay again with his friend at Oxenhope. A path leading across the moor linked the village to Haworth and it was there where Charlotte and Arthur met away from the still critical eyes of Patrick. Being January, the wind was often biting and Charlotte's tiny frame felt the cold more than most. However, bad weather now didn't bother her. She knew Arthur loved her. That had been obvious from the day he had first proposed, but she had to be sure that she could make the marriage work.

Having spent all her adulthood denouncing those who married for anything but love and extolling the virtues of single women who made their own world, she was now on the brink of making the biggest U-turn of her entire life.

Charlotte mentally made a list of the pros and more importantly the cons. She didn't love Arthur. He had no great intellect. He lacked imagination. Marrying him may well mean sacrificing her own identity. There were no guarantees that she could be both a wife and an author. Her friend, the novelist Elizabeth Gaskell, had already warned her that if she did marry Arthur, she might as well put Currer Bell into retirement. While she herself was married, she knew how difficult it was for a woman in the Victorian age to be both an intellectual and a spouse. If Charlotte had any more great ideas for novels, she should get them down on paper now, for once she was married she was unlikely to write anything substantial again. Whichever way she looked at it, a union seemed to go against her sense of integrity and the independence she had spent all her life fighting to preserve. However, even when Charlotte had analysed every negative, every downside, she still came to the same conclusion. She wanted to be Arthur's wife.

Now in her mid thirties the idealistic principles of her childhood finally seemed naïve.

When she had rejected Henry Nussey she told herself that she could only marry a man who she was willing to die for. Life had taught her that such romantic notions were only for the young or her own fictional creations. The respect she had for Arthur might one day turn to love. If it didn't, maybe respect alone was enough.

As Charlotte became convinced her future lay with a man who had turned up in Haworth with no great fanfare, Arthur returned to his duties at Kirk Smeaton and she was left alone to iron out any doubts which remained. Having not been party to Arthur's heartfelt declarations of love, Patrick was unable to share his daughter's optimism. However, much to Charlotte's relief she and Ellen were once again friends. Now more than ever she felt the need to explain her actions to someone who knew her perhaps better than anyone else.

"Papa's consent is gained – this his respect, I believe is won, for Mr Nicholls has in all things proved himself disinterested and

Ever since she was a child, Charlotte had dreamed of fleeing the parsonage for exotic lands and exciting adventures. Now she realised that it was the only place she had ever been truly happy.

forbearing. He has shown, too, that while his feelings are exquisitely keen – he can freely forgive. Certainly I must respect him, nor can I withhold from him more than mere cool respect. In fact, dear Ellen, I am engaged…What seemed at one time impossible is now arranged, and papa begins really to take a pleasure in the prospect. For myself, dear Ellen, why thankful to the One who seems to have guided me through much difficulty, much deep distress and perplexity of mind, I am still very calm, very inexpectant. What I taste of happiness is of the sobrest order. I trust to love my husband – I am grateful for his tender love to me. I believe him to be an affectionate, a conscientious, a high-principled man; and if, with all this, I should yield to regrets, that fine talents, congenial tastes and thoughts are not added, it seems to me I should be most presumptuous and thankless. Providence offers me this destiny. Doubtless then it is best for me."

It was another four months after their meetings on the windswept moor before Arthur finally returned to Haworth. When he did he probably couldn't help but be reminded of the tale of the Prodigal Son. Patrick didn't quite get out the fatted calf, but neither did he shun his future son-in-law. He knew shouting would not change Charlotte's mind and besides, she had given him assurances that he wouldn't be abandoned. The three of them would live together at the parsonage and his daughter had already planned various improvements and changes which would give each as much space as they needed.

"I find myself what people call engaged…I could almost cry sometimes that in this important action of my life I cannot better satisfy papa's perhaps natural pride. My destiny will not be brilliant, certainly, but Mr Nicholls is conscientious, affectionate, pure in heart and life. He offers a most constant and tried attachment — I am very grateful to him. I mean to try to make him happy, and papa too."

Throughout her life, Charlotte had always striven for what others would have dismissed as unattainable. As a governess she wanted her own school. As a writer she wanted fame and critical adoration. But none of that had made her truly happy. She had gone to Brussels and she had gone to London in search of the one thing which might make her feel whole. Now she realised happiness, or at the very least contentment, had been there on her own doorstep and she was ready to embrace it.

Currer Bell and Charlotte Brontë were about to become Mrs Arthur Nicholls.

5. A Life More Ordinary

"Those who have courage to love,
Should have courage to suffer."
Anthony Trollope

Like most brides, Charlotte woke early on the morning of her wedding. She could feel the start of what she was sure was a cold, but this was one time she wasn't going to let illness disturb her plans. It had only been two months since she had accepted Arthur's proposal and she still couldn't quite believe that in a matter of hours she would be a married woman. In truth she had hoped for a little more time to get used to the idea. However, Arthur had understandably not been keen on a long engagement. Fearing that given chance for further contemplation his fiancée might very well change her mind he had been determined they would be man and wife by the end of the summer. When a date had been set for that July, for the first time in months Charlotte had found time to think about something other than Arthur and her father. When she did she realised that in the whirlwind of her own personal life, she had neglected many of those closest to her. With a need to ensure the friends of her past wished her well for the future, she had headed first to Manchester to stay with Elizabeth Gaskell and returned via Ellen's home at Bookroyd. She had talked openly about the doubts which still plagued her, but had insisted she and Arthur could be and would be happy. Charlotte had expected to be grilled on the reason for her apparently sudden change of heart and she wasn't disappointed. Ellen struggled to comprehend how her friend could have fallen for a man she had always dismissed as dull and inferior. By the time Charlotte had left, Ellen was no closer to understanding, but every question she had asked had been honestly answered and she didn't doubt that Charlotte truly believed her future happiness depended on her marriage to Arthur.

When Charlotte had returned to Haworth it was the middle of May. Comforted in the knowledge that for all Ellen's misgivings their friendship was as strong as ever, she had hoped to enjoy her last few months as a single woman. However, plans for the wedding had been brought forward. With Arthur returning as curate, his replacement George de Renzy had been handed his notice. George's spell in Haworth had been both short and inauspicious. Patrick had never hid the fact his new curate fell short in both character and dedication to his predecessor and faced with having to find a new position George had made it clear he was unwilling to stay on any longer than absolutely necessary. It was decided then that Charlotte and Arthur would marry in June.

Both had agreed the wedding would be a quiet, simple affair. However, it wasn't long before every waking moment had become consumed by talk and plans for the marriage. Workmen had already started converting a small room in the back of the house, which had once been home to the Brontës' pet geese Victoria and Albert, into

Charlotte insisted her marriage was to be a simple affair and in a letter detailing the purchase of her wedding dress and veil she wrote:"If I must make a fool of myself it shall be on an economical plain."

a study for Arthur. Charlotte, determined her husband should not feel like an unwanted guest, had taken charge of the decoration. It was she who decided on the green and white curtains and it was she who had the furniture arranged just how she hoped Arthur would like it.

The house had been busier than Patrick had ever remembered it and among the many deliveries and parcels which had arrived each day, few had born his name.

For Charlotte there never seemed enough hours in the day. There had been material for her dress to choose, a never-ending pile of sewing and invitations to write and send. There were only to be a handful of guests at the service, but the wedding breakfast was planned as a more inclusive affair. As the weeks had ticked by, Charlotte who had always maintained she had little interest in the frippery of such occasions had suddenly become a difficult woman to please. The envelopes for the invites had been deemed too big; the design not quite what she asked for and when she realised the white sealing wax she had chosen to match the cards had been forgotten, the rest of the house had soon known about it. Caught up in the irrational frenzy which brides throughout history have come to know so well, Charlotte's temper was shorter than any had remembered seeing it before.

Arthur had done his best to help. While still living in Kirk Smeaton, he had visited Charlotte whenever he could. Some would have been glad to share the burden, but not Charlotte. Arthur couldn't sew, he failed to share her concerns about the invites and his unshakable happy demeanour had only served as a further irritant. When he had written offering to stay in Haworth for a full week to help her with any last minute jobs, he might have imagined his bride-to-be would have been delighted by the plan. Not Charlotte. She had replied immediately and told him that such a long visit really wouldn't be necessary.

Arthur only cared that he and Charlotte were married in the eyes of God. Charlotte wanted that too, but she also wanted the tablecloth for the reception to be right and her dress to fit correctly. Neither she had suspected were Arthur's particular forte.

There had also been her finances to sort. Charlotte was by no means a rich woman. The money she had earned from her books and the investments George had kindly made on her behalf in various railway schemes had left her with a small nest egg of £1,678. The Married Women's Property Act, which would give women control of their assets, was still some decades away and when she said 'I do' it wouldn't be just her heart Charlotte would give to Arthur. On marriage what little wealth she had would be immediately and automatically merged with her husband's.

Charlotte, who had grown up silently reciting the mantra that future security depended on financial independence, was about to give it all away. There was nothing she could do about it, but there was something she could do to ensure her own father didn't lose out.

Drawing up a marriage settlement, a clause was carefully and deliberately inserted stating should she die childless and before Arthur, Patrick would receive a lump sum equivalent to the amount she had earned as a single woman. If Arthur had any complaints, they aren't recorded. He had already said he wanted to marry Charlotte Brontë the person not Charlotte Brontë the author. Her fame and possible future earnings meant little to him. If anyone had doubted his intentions, the marriage settlement stood as proof of his integrity.

Despite a dislike of extravagance, Charlotte did make some concessions to tradition with her dress and wedding bonnet, and those who saw her described her as looking like a snowdrop.

The paperwork was laborious, but as Charlotte had been putting in place all the necessary legal documents for her own wedding to go ahead, she discovered one of her once closest allies and supporters had already raised a toast to his new bride. George it emerged had been happily married for two months. While she imagined his wedding had been a great deal more lavish than her own would be, there was no pang of regret, just a realisation of how far she had grown apart, not just from him, but from London and all it had once promised. Her life was now in Haworth. Her future was with Arthur.

With the marriage ceremony due to start at eight o' clock, the house was busy from dawn. Arthur had stayed the previous evening with his friend in Oxenhope and as he walked across the moor, treading the same path and past the same green hills where he had first convinced his bride to accept his heartfelt proposal, Charlotte began to get ready. She had deliberately chosen a plain outfit. The dress was made of white muslin not silk, the white bonnet, while edged with green leaves had no fancy ribbons and the mantle which covered her shoulders was made of simple white lace. Charlotte was thirty-eight-years-old and she had no desire to wear a gown designed for a much younger bride.

As she had said herself, "If I must make a fool of myself it shall be on an economical plain." Extravagance had no part to play in this particular wedding.

Arthur had kept his promise of keeping the service as secret and as low key as possible, but word soon got round. Those who heard the news in time gathered outside the church. They had seen Charlotte many times before, but dressed all in white most agreed that now she looked as fragile as a snowdrop. It was a more accurate description than any of them ever knew. Delicate and yet resilient, Charlotte might have looked so slight that the gentlest gust of wind could blow her away, but she had survived her fair share of heartbreak and each new adversity had made her grow stronger.

The kind looks from those well-meaning strangers made her feel uncomfortable. Even on her wedding day, Charlotte disliked being the centre of attention, but knowing two of her best friends were by her side gave her strength throughout. Charlotte had asked Ellen to be her bridesmaid as soon as she had announced her engagement. She knew her friend would never be convinced that Arthur was a suitable husband, but she needed her support. It wasn't easy for Ellen. Whatever Charlotte said, she knew that when they walked back up the aisle and out into the churchyard, their friendship would never be quite the same again. For as long as Ellen could remember, whenever Charlotte had a problem she was the one she had turned to. They had shared everything, but now her friend had a new confidant, a new person to rely on. However, for that one day Ellen carried out her duties with no complaints and whatever unkind thoughts she had about Arthur remained unspoken. Charlotte's only other guest was Margaret Wooler. Her friend and one-time teacher had arrived in Haworth with Ellen the evening before the wedding. Margaret had never married, but quite unexpectedly she discovered she was to play a far bigger role in her friend's wedding than she had ever imagined.

Having given his consent to the marriage, Patrick's health had improved a little. Happy to keep in the background and uninterested with the logistics of the day, he had quietly resigned himself to living in the same house with Arthur. Charlotte felt sure that given time friendly relations between her father and her husband would eventually be restored, but Patrick had one last bombshell to drop.

The night before the wedding, Charlotte and her father had gathered as usual to say prayers. They were joined by Ellen and Margaret. Each bowed their heads and closed their eyes, the silent intentions of one directly in conflict with another. Did Ellen pray her friend would see sense and call off the marriage before it was too late? Did Charlotte pray her faith in Arthur would be repaid and those who scorned him forced to humbly apologise? Patrick's intentions, however, had soon become clear. After the final Amen he had announced he was sadly too ill to attend his daughter's wedding. He had, he told them, checked for guidance and in his absence it would in the eyes of the Church be perfectly acceptable for Margaret to give Charlotte away. Patrick's reluctance to play the father of the bride had come as no great surprise. Having broken his will and secured his reluctant approval, Charlotte knew just how difficult the last few months had been for her father.

Patrick had already swallowed his pride to give his consent to the marriage. To Charlotte, that was worth more than the act of formally giving her away, but when she went to bed knowing that when she said her vows a few hours later, the only surviving member of her family would not be there to hear them she couldn't help but wonder how different things might have been.

When the small wedding party left the parsonage the following morning, Patrick retreated to his study. They were met at the church by the Rev Sutcliffe Sowden, a friend of Arthur's from Hebden Bridge, who had agreed to perform the brief service. In less than half an hour, the vows had been said, good wishes had been passed to the happy couple and the registry, witnessed by Ellen and Margaret, had been signed. It was eighteen months since Arthur had first stood in front of Charlotte and asked her to marry him. It had felt like a lifetime, but as he had told himself on many occasions the good things in life were most definitely worth waiting for. Arthur walked back up the lane a husband, his dearly beloved Charlotte now his wife.

The parsonage, which throughout Charlotte's childhood had only had rows of books to soften the pale walls, was now decked out with flowers. The Brontë servants Tabby and Martha, with a little help from Ellen, had busied themselves with the arrangements and even Charlotte had to admit the flowers brought some much needed colour to the place. Soon the house was full, mostly with friends and colleagues of Arthur. As the guests tucked into plates of boiled ham and freshly baked bread some had cause to notice that despite his professed ill health, Patrick did an admirable job of being the life and soul of the party. Charlotte didn't mind and had a stranger happened to pass by the house that day, they would have seen nothing to suggest this was anything other than a simple party in celebration of two newlyweds. However, the most telling thing of all about the marriage was not Patrick's absence at the service, it was the wedding certificate. Next to Arthur's name in the column marked profession was written clerk. In the same column next to Charlotte's name a line had been drawn. On the morning of June 29, 1854, her lifetime's achievements had been cancelled in a single stroke.

A new chapter had begun. Charlotte was now Arthur's wife and while her books were still being avidly read up and down the country, the woman who wrote them was embarking on a very different journey to the one she had lovingly crafted for her own heroines.

As the plates were being cleared, Charlotte went upstairs to

The marriage certificate of
Arthur Nicholls and
Charlotte Brontë.

1854. Marriage solemnized at *Haworth* in the *Parish* of *Bradford* in the County of *York*

No.	When Married	Name and Surname	Age	Condition	Rank or Profession	Residence at the Time of Marriage	Father's Name and Surname	Rank or Profession of Father
346	June 29th	Arthur Bell Nicholls	full age	Bachelor	Clerk	Kirk Smeaton	William Nicholls	Farmer
		Charlotte Brontë	full age	Spinster	―	Haworth	Patrick Brontë	Clerk.

Married in the *Church of Haworth* according to the Rites and Ceremonies of the *Established Church* by me, *Sutcliffe Sowden*
Curate

This Marriage was solemnized between us, { Arthur Bell Nicholls / Charlotte Brontë } in the Presence of us, { Ellen Nussey / Margaret Wooler } change.

Arthur had long been desperate to show her the Ireland where he had grown up and the family he had left behind and they were to leave on honeymoon that day. Returning in a brand new mauve silk dress, which she had ordered a few weeks earlier from Halifax, she took Arthur's arm and together they said their farewells.

Charlotte had as many doubts about visiting Ireland as she'd had about the wedding. She didn't want to dampen Arthur's obvious excitement about returning home, but all she imagined about her Celtic cousins suggested it was going to be more of a trial for her than a holiday. While her own father had been born there, he'd had the good fortune to escape and like most English people, she was convinced that while the fields of Athenry were only a few miles away across the Irish Sea it was a world away from what anyone would call civilisation.

Before Charlotte was forced to confront her own prejudices, she and Arthur stopped en route in Wales. Their wedding night was spent in Conway. The weather was miserable, Charlotte's cold had worsened, but nothing could detract from the beauty of what she saw before her. She had seen dramatic scenery in the Lake District and the moors above Haworth had, until the death of her sister Emily, been the source of constant delight, but the valleys of Snowdonia were something else altogether. After all the build up to the wedding, it was good to be away from home. With rarely another soul around, she no longer needed to worry what anyone else thought about her marriage and the burden of other people's expectations began to lift.

By the time she and Arthur set sail to Dublin a few days later she was still worried about what strange places she would find across the water and wondered how long she would have to stay without appearing rude, but she was in a much better mood.

They were met in Ireland by Arthur's brother who was manager of the Grand Canal. The waterway, which had provided links between the city and Banagher and Limerick, had been largely responsible for transforming the region's economic fortunes and as the man now in charge, Charlotte's brother-in-law commanded much respect. When Arthur's two cousins who completed the welcome party also disappointedly failed to live up to her image of Irish barbarians running wild on a diet of whiskey, Charlotte began to think that maybe, just maybe, she might have to revise her opinions of the Emerald Isle. Arthur had much he wanted to show his wife. Avoiding the north side of the city, which had gone into decline, the once proud Georgian town houses turned into slums, they instead took a tour round Trinity College where Arthur had begun his studies some twenty years or so before. Opposite the Irish Houses of Parliament, it was a university steeped in history. Arthur showed Charlotte the chapel, the museum and the library which was the pride of Dublin. Home to the Book of Kells and a treasure trove of first editions, for a book lover like Charlotte it was a little piece of heaven.

Normally she would have happily spent hours wandering the aisles, soaking up the atmosphere of quiet, studious reflection, but now suffering quite badly from the cold, they were forced to curtail their sightseeing. If Arthur was disappointed he didn't show it, besides they had the rest of their lives to share each other's loves and passions and he knew even more impressive sights awaited them.

The next stop was Cuba House in Banagher on the banks of the River Shannon. It was the home of his late uncle who had raised

Arthur and his brother when their own parents had died. Arthur had told Charlotte tales from his childhood, but she somehow couldn't quite marry his stories of Ireland with what she knew of her father's own upbringing in the same country in abject poverty. Like Patrick, Arthur had been born into a poor farming family. Had he not been orphaned at an early age, he would have likely been forced to plough the same unfortunate furrow. However, in the care of his uncle, Dr Alan Bell, headmaster of the renowned Royal School, his fate had taken a very different path.

Driving through the wrought-iron gates and down the driveway lined with lime trees, Charlotte realised Arthur's Ireland was not the same one her own ancestors knew. Branagher had boasted one of the biggest corn markets in all of Ireland and while it was moving into tougher economic times, the wealth it had attracted was still very much visible.

From the outside Cuba House, which stood in front of the boarding school and classrooms buildings, looked, said Charlotte, like a real gentleman's country seat. Inside was no less disappointing. There was space, so much space. Even the corridors seemed wider than the whole of the ground floor of the parsonage and the high ceilings and spacious drawing rooms leant a lofty grandeur to the place. Empty, it felt too big for any ordinary family, but when the peat fires were lit and the rooms were full of Arthur's many cousins, the grand building was at once transformed into a welcoming home. It was also, Charlotte was pleased to note, neat and tidy and much to her surprise full of "English order and repose".

There were so many people to meet and Arthur's relations, many of whom had already read her books, were eager to get to know the latest addition to their family. They wanted to tell Charlotte how much they had enjoyed *Jane Eyre*, they wanted to hear from her what life was like in Yorkshire and the famous people she had met in London. Once they had finished with their many questions, they also wanted to tell her just how well she had done for herself by marrying Arthur. Even the servants talked about him as being "one of the best gentlemen in the country".

It was all a little overwhelming. Arthur's aunt, the widow of his late uncle, saw that she was unwell and while she had many things she wanted to ask and many stories to share, she also knew that Charlotte needed rest. Within a few days, Charlotte's health was much improved, the cough had all but gone and colour had returned to her cheeks. Mrs Bell took much of the credit for her guest's recovery, but there was something else which had helped Charlotte from her sick bed. In his own country, mixing with those who knew him long before he became a curate in Haworth, Charlotte had begun to see Arthur in an entirely new light. The last few months had been emotionally exhausting for both of them. She knew her father and Ellen were still wary of her new husband and were waiting for him to make a mistake, which would give them grounds to say 'I told you so'. If only, she thought, they could have seen him as she did now. Charlotte knew she had made the right decision. She might not have yet loved Arthur, but as she journeyed with him across Ireland her affection for him was definitely growing.

Leaving Banagher amid promises they would return in the near future and extending invites to Haworth, Arthur and Charlotte travelled on to Limerick and Kilkee in County Clare. The first hotel they had booked fell far short of the high standard of hospitality they had enjoyed at Cuba House. It didn't matter. Charlotte had fallen in love with the ocean view. Ever since she had first been to

Scarborough, the sea had held a powerful attraction and the "wild iron-bound coast" she now looked out on was even more dramatic. She would have happily spent her entire day watching the "waves battling at the rocks" and looking on as the occasional seagull swooped into land.

Arthur may have only been married to Charlotte a few weeks, but he knew when she wanted to be left alone and his sensitivity surprised her.

"The first morning we went out onto the cliffs and saw the Atlantic coming in all white foam," she wrote to Ellen. "I did not know whether I should get leave or time to take the matter in my own way. I did not want to talk – but I did want to look and be silent. Having hinted a petition, licence was not refused – covered with a rug to keep off the spray I was allowed to sit where I chose – and he only interrupted when he thought I crept too near the edge of the cliff. So far he is always good in this way – and this protection which does not interfere or pretend is I believe a thousand times better than any half sort of psuedo sympathy. I will try with God's help to be as indulgent to him whenever indulgence is needed."

As they moved onto Tarbert and then to Tralee, Charlotte and Arthur soaked up the scenery, not knowing when, if ever, they would return. In Killarney they hired horses to ride through the Gap of Dunloe. The narrow seven-mile pass which wended its way past five small lakes before descending in the Black Valley was a popular tourist spot.

It was also notoriously treacherous. Feeling sure she would be able to navigate the broken path, Charlotte ignored their guide's advice to dismount. Unfortunately her horse was not so confident. Unnerved after stumbling on the rough terrain, it reared and

Charlotte was thrown onto the stones below. Arthur jumped off his own horse and grabbed the reins. Lying underneath, Charlotte saw the horse kick. It missed her by only the smallest of margins. When she was finally pulled to her feet she felt only a little minor bruising but an intense feeling of gratitude.

More than a little relieved to be moving on to Glengarrif and Cork, the days sped by and it was not long before they arrived back in Dublin. Ireland had been an eye-opening experience, there were views and people she would remember forever and she understood now why Arthur talked so fondly of his past. However, home for Charlotte was Haworth. They had been gone a month. She missed the familiarity of the house and unable to check on her father's health for herself, she missed him too. Arthur would have happily stayed longer, but the honeymoon was over. Mr and Mrs Nicholls returned to Yorkshire.

With the lush hills of Ireland but memories and her new relations hundreds of miles away, Charlotte found she quickly slipped into a routine. While she had once been Charlotte Brontë during the day and Currer Bell at night, now she was a curate's wife twenty-four hours a day.

Arthur who had gained a little weight during their honeymoon and who looked much healthier than he had done in months returned to his duties with great dedication. Each morning without fail he could be found at the National School in which he had always taken so much pride. To be finally back where he had always felt he belonged was a source of much personal and professional pride. For an hour and a half or more he would instruct his pupils in the Christian teachings, setting them, he hoped, on a path to moral righteousness. Outside of the classroom he was equally busy. The

Charlotte fell in love with the dramatic landscapes of Ireland. She had less happy memories of the Gap of Dunloe where she was thrown from her horse. (Courtesy of Fáilte Ireland)

pile of paperwork never seemed to get any smaller and should he find a quiet moment it was usually quickly filled by one of the parishioners wanting his advice or to share with him their latest woes. Most afternoons were spent visiting the sick and in Haworth there was no shortage of illness. The Babbage Report four years earlier had highlighted the squalid conditions in which many of the town's nearly seven thousand residents lived. Improvements to the sewerage and drainage system were beginning to be made, but it would take much longer for the mortality statistics to reflect the changes.

While her husband was out, Charlotte had her own list of duties to complete. In truth they were much the same as they were before she was married, but now she enjoyed her part in achieving domestic bliss. A few years earlier she would have viewed tea with the church bell ringers or supper with the Sunday school teachers as a necessary evil. Now she took pleasure in meeting those, who like her husband were a cornerstone of the community. A party for five hundred guests was organised in the schoolroom. It was Arthur's idea, a way of thanking those who had been so keen to pass on their best wishes to the newly married couple and who had stood by him when times had not been so good. The party was evidence of Arthur's general decency and proved to Charlotte that her assessment of him had been right.

There may have been little intellectual stimulus in keeping the house clean and attending to Arthur's needs, but amid the general distractions of the Church and married life Charlotte found a quiet contentment. When she described those first weeks back in Haworth, it was as always an honest portrayal. There were moments she admitted when she craved to be alone, moments when she wondered what had happened to her old self, but she always insisted she never had any regrets.

"The colour of my thoughts are a good deal changed," she told Ellen just a month after her honeymoon. "I know more of the realities of life than I once did. I think many false ideas are propagated perhaps unintentionally...Take warning Ellen, the married woman can call but a very small portion of each day her own. Not that I complain of this sort of monopoly as yet and I hope I never shall incline to regard it as a misfortune, but it certainly exists."

Aside from Arthur there was also her father to look after. Patrick was now seventy-eight-years-old and frail. His son-in-law had kept his promise to further ease his preaching duties and Charlotte now tended to his every need. She had always known that as a married woman she would have little time to devote to writing and without the promise of new work, interest in her would inevitably die down. The decision to step back from the world of literature had been hers and hers alone. She now had a new challenge. She wanted domestic comfort, she wanted a happy marriage and if that meant giving up her fame and her writing career, it was a sacrifice she was more than willing to make.

"My own life is more occupied than it used to be," she told her friend Margaret Wooler. "I have not so much time for thinking: I am obliged to be more practical, for my dear Arthur is a very practical as well as a very punctual, methodical man...I believe it is not bad for me that his bent should be so wholly towards matters of real life and active usefulness – so little inclined to the literary and contemplative."

So convinced was she that marriage had saved her from a life of lonely unhappiness, she decided to see if she could find Ellen a suitable husband. Rev Sowden found himself at the top of the list of likely candidates. Charlotte felt sure if they could only spend a few days in each other's company, love or at the very least mutual respect would blossom. When Ellen visited that autumn, Arthur invited his friend and Charlotte turned matchmaker. When they went walking on the moors, she did her best to ensure that Ellen and Rev Sowden had time to get to know each other. There was no room for subtlety, but for all Charlotte's efforts it came to nothing. Ellen had seemed interested, but Rev Sowden, who was scraping by a living as a curate, never showed the faintest glimmer of attraction to Charlotte's best friend. Ellen was resolved to remain single and when she saw the influence Arthur was exerting over her friend she was glad to be so.

Arthur had always been uneasy of his wife's fame and the unwanted attention it might bring. While he had seen how even the most gentlest criticism of her books had caused her pain, he believed the literary press was the least of Charlotte's worries. He was convinced that unscrupulous types were poised ready to sully her name and reputation and he saw it as his job to stop them. Glancing over her shoulder one day he caught her writing to Ellen. Charlotte was telling her about the peculiar behaviour of another friend who for some reason best known to herself seemed intent on befriending one of her husband's former flames. It was exactly the kind of idle gossip Arthur felt could be dangerous in the wrong hands.

Like many men he only wrote letters of a practical nature and he couldn't understand why anyone would want to spend their time debating who might be doing what and to whom. He was, however, sensible enough to know there was little chance of persuading his wife round to his way of thinking.

However, if he couldn't prevent Charlotte writing, he grew

Arthur in the house some of the long absent happiness returned. Christmas was once again something to celebrate.

It says much about how comfortable she felt with Arthur that she even teased him about her writing or rather lack of it. One winter evening as the wind howled round the parsonge, they were sat as they often did talking about nothing very much in particular. The conversation turned to books. Her husband had never been a particularly avid reader, preferring The Churchman's Companion or his book of Practical Sermons to any work of fiction and Charlotte joked that had it not been for him she would no doubt have finished another novel by now. Had he not, she told him, pursued her so doggedly she imagined critics might currently have been championing or pulling apart her latest work. To prove the point, she rushed upstairs and returned with pages of an unfinished manuscript. That evening Arthur enjoyed a rare private reading of her work.

Emma, as the incomplete book was titled, told of a child sent to boarding school by an apparently wealthy father. The headmistress, a woman impressed by money and little else, lavished attention on the child she believed to have been born of the very best stock. However, when the father vanished, leaving fees unpaid the headmistress proved not quite so accommodating. Abandoned by all those she thought she could trust, the girl's only hope lay with an eccentric bachelor intent on getting to the bottom of her troubled past.

Arthur was quick to point out that her choice of setting, yet another school, may well cause readers to accuse of her of repetition. It didn't matter, Charlotte was never going to finish the book. *Jane Eyre*, *Shirley*, *Villette* and even the unpublished *The Professor* had been born from long periods of introspection. They had been inspired by heartbreak and written against the backdrop of tragedy. Now Charlotte was content, the emotional extremes which had fuelled her writing had been tempered.

The winter had been harsh that year and Charlotte had been forced to spend much of her time indoors. When the snow finally began to melt, she and Arthur grabbed an opportunity to see a nearby waterfall in full force. It was an impressive sight and they stood for a while to admire the white torrent pounding over the rocks. However, the weather on the moors has never made concessions to the unprepared sightseer and true to form the heavens opened. By the time they got back to the parsonage both Charlotte and Arthur were drenched. They quickly changed out of their wet clothes, but the next day Charlotte felt the familiar signs of a winter chill. In the past she might have bemoaned her bad fortune, but not now. Cold or no cold, she said she would not have missed the spectacle for the world.

Thankfully the cold didn't take hold, but it wasn't long after that she discovered there was a much greater threat to her health. Charlotte was pregnant. The earliest signs had been easy to ignore, but as the weeks turned into months she could feel her body changing By the middle of January she was all but certain that she was with child.

"My health has been really very good ever since my return from Ireland till about ten days ago, when the stomach seemed quite suddenly to lose its tone – indigestion and continual faint sickness have been my portion every since," she wrote to Ellen, no doubt wanting to share her fears without yet being able to talk directly about the possibility of pregnancy. "Don't conjecture – dear Nell –

for it is too soon yet — though I certainly never before felt as I have done lately. But keep the matter wholly to yourself — for I can come to no decided opinion at present."

It was little wonder Charlotte was loath to confront the prospect of motherhood. In Haworth, where the average age of death was twenty-five, forty-one per cent of babies didn't reach their first birthday. Some women were lucky, they were robust enough to make it through the nine months, but Charlotte had always been frail. If there was a cold to catch she caught it and while she may have survived her brother and sisters, childbirth was not for the faint of heart or body.

She went into denial. Not wanting to have her worst fears confirmed she refused to see a doctor and whenever Arthur asked how she was feeling she did her best to muster a smile. It wasn't a very convincing mask. They might have called it morning sickness, but the waves of nausea which swept over Charlotte refused to confine themselves to one particular part of the day.

She hoped that given time the sickness would pass, but as Arthur watched his wife as she lay on the sofa unable to walk even a few short yards, he could stand it no more. Charlotte needed to see a doctor. Dr MacTurk who had a surgery in Bradford was contacted and he agreed to travel to Haworth at the first available opportunity. At the end of the consultation Charlotte and Arthur knew for definite that they were expecting their first child. Dr MacTurk's prognosis, such as it was, gave some hope for both mother and child. Her condition he said would be of "some duration", but as it was down to entirely "natural causes" there was no "immediate danger".

However, when Tabby fell ill, complaining of stomach cramps, the parsonage suddenly found itself in the grip of sickness and while no one was sure whether Charlotte had also caught the same infection, her condition worsened. Patrick had always feared his daughter's decision to marry might be the death of her. Charlotte had never expressed any great desire to start a family, but remaining childless was more a matter of good luck than good judgement. His own wife had born him six children, but Charlotte he knew was not so robust. He had buried enough women who had died in labour to know the dangers of pregnancy and hardly able to watch her suffering, he prayed that she would recover.

Charlotte didn't rally. Other mothers-to-be look forward to the time when passersby look at their swelling stomachs and tell them how well they are looking or how much they suit pregnancy. Charlotte couldn't even make it to the front door. Laid in bed, the days and the agonising nights merged into one. Martha took her cups of beef tea, but most went untouched. She couldn't bear the sight or smell of food and even the medicine the doctor had prescribed caused her to wretch.

Valentine's Day came and went. Arthur found it increasingly difficult to reassure Charlotte. He wanted to tell her everything was going to be ok, but he couldn't even convince himself. It was a desperate time and while Charlotte was struggling to sleep, her stomach gripped in agony, Tabby was quietly passing away. When the Brontës' faithful servant had first arrived at the parsonage thirty years before she was already long past her youth. However, age had never seemed to bother her much and she had quickly become a favourite with the young Brontë children. Often found in the kitchen telling stories as she put that evening's mutton onto stew, Tabby had always been much more than a housekeeper. She had watched the children grow up and she had seen and felt the heartache caused by their untimely deaths. For a few years now, she had been unable to carry out many of her usual duties, but she had become part of the family and neither Patrick nor Charlotte would have ever entertained the idea of her living anywhere else. Charlotte barely had the strength to raise her head from the pillow, but when Arthur told her Tabby had gone rapidly downhill she immediately scrawled a note asking the doctor in Haworth to send some medicine. It was no good. A few days later Tabby died. She was eighty-four-years-old. Even if she survived this pregnancy, Charlotte knew she was unlikely to get to Tabby's age and her death reminded her of her own mortality. On that same day Charlotte made her will. There was in truth no need. She owned few assets and she had already ensured that whatever happened to her, Patrick would always be financially secure. However, now the marriage settlement, which she had been so keen to put in place, suddenly felt wrong. Charlotte now trusted Arthur with everything. She trusted him to look after her father even if she was no longer around and should she or her child manage to survive, she knew whatever life threw at them Arthur would always be there to pick up the pieces.

"In case I die without issue I give and bequeath my husband all my property to him absolutely and entirely," she wrote. "But in case I leave issue I bequeath to my husband the interest of my property during his lifetime, and at his death I desire that the principal should go to my surviving child or children; should there be more than one child, share and share alike."

Charlotte was not able to attend Tabby's funeral. Arthur conducted the service and as he said the final prayers and the coffin was lowered into the ground he may well have had cause to glance up to the bedroom window just a few yards away where his own wife was battling to stay alive. He was exhausted. Dividing his time between his wife's bedside, the church and the school, Arthur had barely had time to eat. When occasionally he had dozed off his sleep was often troubled and the worry was visible for all to see, even Charlotte noticed how worn he looked. Arthur tried to put on a brave face, but she knew her illness was hurting him just as much as it was her.

"I'm not going to talk about my sufferings it would be useless and painful," she told Ellen, who was no doubt wondering whether Arthur was looking after her friend as properly as he should.

"I want to give you an assurance which I know will comfort you – and that is that I find my husband the tenderest nurse, the kindest support, the best earthly comfort that ever woman had. His patience never fails and it is tried by sad days and broken nights."

Arthur prayed hard for his wife's recovery and in the March it seemed they had been answered. Charlotte sat up in bed, she looked, if not a picture of health, then certainly less pale than she had done for some weeks. She and Arthur quietly dared to hope that Dr MacTurk had been right all along and that given a few more weeks all would be well. It wasn't. Charlotte's recovery was brief and when the pain returned it was even worse than before. She was soon delirious. When she cried out for food and drink, Martha brought whatever she asked for, but Charlotte was unable to swallow even the smallest morsel.

The hurried note to Ellen, singing the praises of her now very much loved husband, were to be the last words from the hand that had written *Jane Eyre*. Both Arthur and Patrick realised Charlotte only had days to live and there was nothing even the most experienced doctor could do to change the situation.

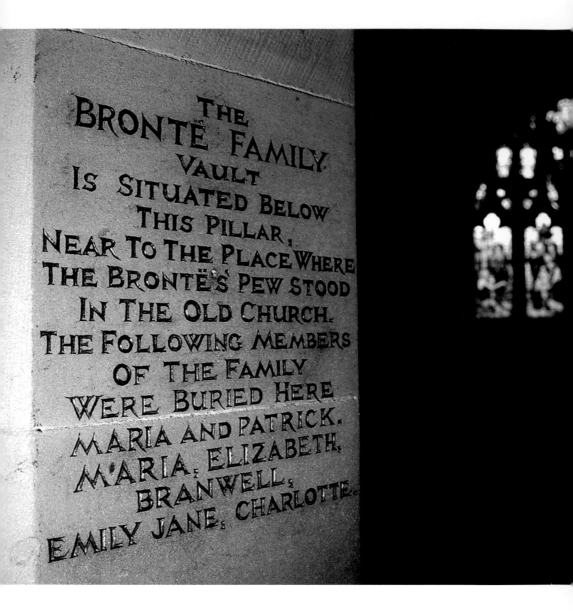

THE
BRONTË FAMILY
VAULT
IS SITUATED BELOW
THIS PILLAR,
NEAR TO THE PLACE WHERE
THE BRONTË'S PEW STOOD
IN THE OLD CHURCH.
THE FOLLOWING MEMBERS
OF THE FAMILY
WERE BURIED HERE
MARIA AND PATRICK.
MARIA, ELIZABETH,
BRANWELL,
EMILY JANE, CHARLOTTE.

A few weeks before her 39th birthday, Charlotte died. Her marriage had lasted less than a year, but after years of dreaming and praying she had finally tasted true happiness.

As she slipped in and out of consciousness, Arthur took up a permanent vigil by his wife's bedside and later he remembered how Charlotte had desperately tried to cling onto life.

"I am not going to die am I?" she had asked him. "He will not separate us, we have been so happy."

Charlotte died on Saturday morning, March 31, 1855. Her unborn baby did not survive.

Throughout her life Charlotte had craved love. Growing up she had dreamed of a whirlwind romance. She had wanted the Duke of Zamorna to take her to Angria, a place full of possibilities. Later she had found Monsieur Heger, a man who had changed her life forever. Without him and the heartache he caused, the world may never have seen *Jane Eyre* or *Villette*. Then there was George, the young good-looking publisher who turned out to be nothing more than a friend. When she had least expected it, Arthur for so long on the fringes of her life had forced his way into her heart. He may not have been the most intelligent or imaginative of men, but in Charlotte's eyes he was far from second best. She had wanted companionship, she had wanted someone to protect her from the outside world she found so difficult to deal with and when things went wrong she wanted someone to reassure her. Charlotte may have spent much of her life yearning for excitement and dreaming of a life of action, but ultimately she wanted security. Arthur gave her that, but he also gave her the one thing no other man in her life ever had – the knowledge that he loved her passionately. The contentment Charlotte found at the end of her life might have been of a very different kind to the one she had gone searching for so many years before, but it was real and constant.

The pursuit of romance overshadowed much of Charlotte's adult

Timeline

1816: Charlotte Brontë, the third daughter of Patrick and Maria Brontë, is born on April 21 at Thornton, near Bradford.

1817: Patrick Branwell Brontë, Charlotte's only brother, is born on June 26.

1818: Emily Jane Brontë is born on July 30.

1820: Anne, the youngest of the Brontë children is born on January 17. In the April, the family move from Thornton to Haworth.

1821: On September 15, Patrick's wife Maria dies from cancer.

1824: In August, Charlotte joins her two elder sisters, Maria and Elizabeth, at the Clergy Daughters' School in Cowan Bridge. By the end of the year, Emily has also become a pupil at the school.

1825: Maria dies in May of tuberculosis. A month later Elizabeth dies of the same disease and Patrick removes Charlotte and Emily from the school. His sister-in-law, Elizabeth Branwell, agrees to move from Cornwall to Haworth to look after the children.

1826: Inspired by a set of toy soldiers bought by Patrick for Branwell, the four Brontë children embark on an epic period of story-telling.

1831: In January, 14-year-old Charlotte is sent to Roe Head School run by Margaret Wooler. It was here she meets lifelong friends Ellen Nussey and Mary Taylor.

1832: In May, Charlotte leaves the school and goes back to Haworth.

1835: Charlotte returns to Roe Head as teacher in July.

1837: Charlotte writes to poet laureate Robert Southey asking his advice about her writing.

1838: In December, Charlotte leaves Roe Head for good.

1839: Ellen's brother Henry proposes to Charlotte in the March. His offer is promptly rejected. Two months later Charlotte becomes a temporary governess for the Sidgwick family who live at Stonegappe, near Skipton. She returns home in the summer and in August, Irish curate David Bryce proposes. Charlotte turns him down.

1841: Charlotte secures another governess position, this time with the White family who live at Rawdon. With plans to open her own

1857: Elizabeth Gaskell's *The Life of Charlotte Brontë* is published to critical acclaim. The first full-length biography of a female novelist proclaimed Charlotte to be a genius and the myth of the Brontës began.

1861: Patrick's health deteriorates and on June 7 following a series of fits he dies at the age of 84.

1864: Having returned to Ireland, Arthur Nicholls marries his cousin Mary Bell.

1906: On December 2, a few weeks before his 88th birthday, Arthur Nicholls dies.

Acknowledgements

Writing can be a solitary pursuit, so thank you to all those who provided invaluable advice, constant support and occasional distraction along the way. In particular Duncan Hamilton and the team at Great Northern for making a dream become a reality. To the Yorkshire Post, the Brontë Society and Fáilte Ireland for opening up their photographic archives and proving that often a picture does tell a thousand words. To Paul for always being there and to Charlotte Brontë for not only living an extraordinary life, but for writing many hundreds of letters the like of which we will probably never see again.

Sources

Selected Letters of Charlotte Brontë, edited by Margaret Smith, Oxford University Press, 2007.

Unquiet Soul, Margot Peters, Hodder and Stoughton, 1975.

The Brontës, Juliet Barker, Phoenix, 1994.

Charlotte Brontë A Passionate Life, Lyndall Gordon, Chatto & Windus, 1994.

The Brontë Story, Margaret Lane, William Heinemann, 1953.

The Word Within: The Brontës at Haworth, Juliet Gardiner, Collins & Brown, 1992.

Tales of Angria, edited by Heather Glen, Penguin Books, 2006.

Jane Eyre, Charlotte Brontë, Everyman edition, 1991.

Villette, Charlotte Brontë, Oxford University Press, 1984.

Shirley, Charlotte Brontë, Oxford University Press, 1987.

The Professor, Charlotte Brontë, Wordsworth Editions, 1998.